W. G. Lyttle was proud to be the owner of the first telephone in Bangor. Photograph courtesy and copyright of A. G. Lyttle.

Daft Eddie

OR,

THE SMUGGLERS OF STRANGFORD LOUGH

A TALE OF KILLINCHY

By W. G. LYTTLE

Author of "Sons of the Sod," "The Adventures of Paddy M'Quillan," "The Adventures of Robin Gordon," "Life in Ballycuddy," "Betsy Gray or Hearts of Down," &c., &c.

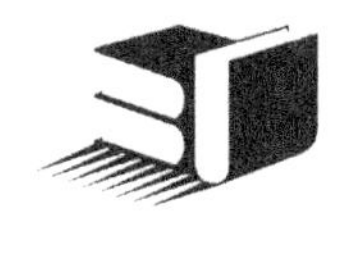

BOOKS ULSTER

First published in 1889.

This new edition published in 2015 by Books Ulster. Text based on the 1914 edition published by R. Carswell of Belfast.

ISBN 978-1-910375-23-5 (Paperback)

ISBN 978-1-910375-24-2 (Kindle)

INTRODUCTION

In the late Nineteenth Century just about everybody in North Down and the Ards peninsula would have known of W. G. Lyttle. He was a provincial newspaper owner and journalist, a raconteur, and a successful author of local interest books. But he is now more than a century dead and relatively few people in the area today have any knowledge of who he was and the legacy he left behind. Stories of great events played out on the world stage and of prominent people who participated in them are taught in our schools, novels of universal appeal are studied, yet local history and literature are all but entirely disregarded, and so people like Lyttle and their works often fall quickly into obscurity. The republication of the six books in this series[1] aims to raise his profile again in the hope that it will generate renewed interest in the man and his writing and encourage some among the current and future generations to reconnect with their cultural heritage. The following is not intended as a comprehensive biography or bibliography of the works of W. G. Lyttle, nor an academic analysis of his writing. It is merely a rudimentary outline sketch designed to whet the appetite for further study and research among those with the time, inclination and ability. The existing biographical and bibliographical information generally available is patchy to say the least and quite possibly inaccurate in parts. It was, for instance, commonly believed until relatively recently that the author's middle name was 'Guard' but, on examining Lyttle's will and other legal documents, Kenneth Robinson, a librarian and local historian, discovered that his name was actually Wesley *Greenhill* Lyttle. Robinson surmised that the error propagated from an error in the *Belfast News-Letter* obituary which confused W. G. Lyttle with a prominent Methodist minister of the time, the Rev. Wesley Guard.

What we *can* be sure of is that Lyttle was born in Newtownards on the 15th April, 1844, and died in Bangor[2] on the 1st November 1896. This is inscribed on his monument which stands in the grounds of Bangor Abbey.[3] The engraved lettering, which is now partially effaced by time and weather, goes on to read:

> "A man of rare natural gifts, he raised himself to a high position among the journalists of Ireland. He was a brilliant and graceful writer, a true humourist and an accomplished poet. Robin was a kind friend, a genial companion and a true son of County Down."

'Robin' was the name he assumed when giving his humorous recitals around the country in the guise of a County Down farmer and by which he became affectionately known. It was the publication of these readings that merited his inclusion in David James O'Donoghue's *The Poets of Ireland* (1912):

> **LYTTLE, WESLEY GUARD.**—Robin's Readings, eight volumes, 18 —.
> Born April 15, 1844, at Newtownards, Co. Down, and self-educated. Was known all over Ulster as "Robin," author of a great number of poems and sketches in the dialect of a Downshire farmer, which he used to give as public readings in that character. These entertainments were enormously popular, and the eight volumes of "Robin's Readings" ran through various editions. Lyttle also published some stories, such as "Sons of the Sod," "The Smugglers of Strangford Lough," and "Betsy Gray, a Tale of '98." He was successively a junior reporter, a school teacher, a lecturer on Dr. Corry's "Irish Diorama," a teacher of shorthand (having been, perhaps, the first to teach it publicly in Belfast), an accountant, a newspaper proprietor, editor, and printer. He started *The*

> *North Down and Bangor Gazette*, a strong Liberal and Home Rule paper, in 1880. He died on November 1, 1896.

It should be noted that O'Donoghue has erroneously given Lyttle's middle name as 'Guard', but there are other inaccuracies and areas of confusion too. Lyttle founded *The North Down Herald* in 1880, extending the title to *The North Down Herald and Bangor Gazette* in 1883 when he moved the newspaper to Bangor in that year. The full title of *The Smugglers of Strangford Lough* is *Daft Eddie or the Smugglers of Strangford Lough*,[4] and *Betsy Gray, a Tale of '98* is more accurately *Betsy Gray; or, Hearts of Down: A Tale of Ninety-eight*; and *Sons of the Sod* is subtitled 'A Tale of County Down'. It is generally accepted today that there are only three volumes of *Robin's Readings—The Adventures of Paddy M'Quillan*, *The Adventures of Robert Gordon* and *Life in Ballycuddy*—but in his Preface to the 1968 *Mourne Observer* edition of *Betsy Gray* Aiken McClelland states that these humorous monologues were issued in eight pamphlets after being previously published in the *North Down Herald*. However, Mark Thompson, a Lyttle enthusiast from Ballyhalbert, recently unearthed some advertisements from the *Belfast News-Letter* which indicate that at least part of the series was first published in *The Newry Telegraph* as early as 1878. From the *News-Letter* issue of January 6th 1879 comes the following:

> *The Newry Telegraph*, published on Tuesday, Thursday and Saturday, is on sale, every morning of publication, at Miss Henderson's, Castle Place, Belfast. The *Telegraph* of Saturday last contained No. 4 of *Paddy M'Quillan's Trip tae Glesgow*. A few copies of 1, 2, and 3 may also still be had.

It is perfectly possible that Lyttle did print what later formed the basis for *Robin's Readings* in the *North Down Herald* but copies of the newspaper are unavailable to check. The British Library only holds the first five issues. No trace of the eight pamphlets mentioned by Aiken McClelland has as yet been found. The story 'The Newtownards Mileeshy' by 'Robin', which was afterwards included in *The Adventures of Robert Gordon* (Part 2 of *Robin's Readings*), appeared in the *Newtownards Chronicle* in three parts during April 1879 and was advertised as 'from his forthcoming *Humorous Readings*'.[5] The second volume was published in Belfast by Allen and Johnston in 1880. A second edition of *Humorous Readings* by 'Robin' was published in 1886. It appears that Lyttle produced his own 'Author's Edition' in 3 volumes as the National Library of Ireland holds Vol. 3, *Life in Ballycuddy* (1892) in its collections. The excellent *A Guide to Irish Fiction 1650-1900* (2006) by Loeber & Loeber refers to a Belfast edition of *Robin's Readings* published by Joseph Blair in 3 volumes in 1893, copies of which are stated to be held at the University of Kansas. R. Carswell & Son of Queen Street, Belfast, also published *Robin's Readings* in 3 volumes, bound in illustrated paper wrappers, in the early part of the 20th Century, but just to add to the confusion they included *Sons of the Sod* as part of the *Robin's Readings* series. They also seem to have mistakenly put the author's initials as 'W. C.' rather than 'W. G.' on at least two of the covers. In a later hardback edition, generally bound in green or blue cloth cloth, Carswell included *The Adventures of Paddy M'Quillan*, *The Adventures of Robert Gordon* and *Life in Ballycuddy* in the one volume, but correctly excluded *Sons of the Sod*.

Some tenacious detective work would be required to properly unravel the publication history of *Robin's Readings*, but there is no doubt that the stories included derived from the texts of Lyttle's recitals and that they were first published in collected form as *Humorous Readings* by 'Robin', although the content varied and the text was revised between editions.

There is a degree of confusion too over the chronology of Lyttle's later publications. Rolf and Magda Loeber in *A Guide to*

Irish Fiction have it tentatively as *The Bangor Season. What's to be seen and how to see it* (1885), *Sons of the Sod: A Tale of County Down* (1886), *Betsy Gray; or, Hearts of Down: A Tale of Ninety-eight* (1888) and *Daft Eddie or the Smugglers of Strangford Lough* (c.1890), but, apart from *Sons of the Sod*, they could not locate a first edition of any of them. An abridged edition of *The Bangor Season* was published in Belfast by Appletree Press in 1976. *Sons of the Sod* was republished in Bangor by the author's son in 1911 and again c. 1915 by Carswell in Belfast. In 2005 Books Ulster reproduced it as No. 2 in the 'Ulster-Scots Classics' series. An 'Author's Edition' of *Betsy Gray* was published in 1894 and many subsequent editions were produced after that, including a number by Carswell in the early 20th Century and one by the *Mourne Observer*, with an informative, illustrated appendix, in 1968. Another edition, published by Ullans Press in 2008 (No. 4 in the 'Ulster-Scots Classics' series) included an essay on Lyttle and Betsy Gray by Kenneth Robinson. In that he identified the serialization of the book in the *North Down Herald* as beginning on Saturday 7th November 1885. *Daft Eddie*, which according to Robinson was serialized in the *Herald* in 1889, was re-published in an undated edition by Carswell and then in 1979 by the *Mourne Observer*, again with an illustrated appendix. Kenneth Robinson has noted similarities between Lyttle's *Daft Eddie* and a story *The Merry Hearts of Down; A Tale of Killinchy and the Ards* that appeared in issues of the *Newtownards Independent* under the name of 'Rev. J. B.' in February to May 1872. Lyttle also published *Lyttle's North Down Almanac and Directory* from 1880 to 1894.

W. G. Lyttle's performances and stories were extremely popular in their day, especially, of course, in North Down and the Ards. *Robin's Readings* produced no end of amusement because Lyttle (as Robin) was affectionately mimicking the way the locals spoke and put his fictional characters into all sorts of laughter-provoking situations. Even in his more serious books, like *Sons of the Sod* and *Betsy Gray* there are elements of comedy drawn from the dialect and innocence of the common folk. Rather than taking umbrage at being aped in this way and having fun poked at them, they seemed to delight in the celebrity. They understood that Lyttle's intention was not to be condescending or malicious, but that his representations derived from a deep love for the people and their language. The purpose was not to have a joke at their expense, but rather to be a joke in which all could share.

Another reason for his enormous success was that in *Sons of the Sod*, *Betsy Gray* and *Daft Eddie* Lyttle touched on subjects of great interest to the local population. The places, people and events mentioned in his books were obviously very familiar to the community and it therefore identified with them. Historical accuracy was not a primary concern for the author. He was a showman and a salesman first and foremost and, as the saying goes, he would not let the facts get in the way of a good story. Nevertheless, if nothing else, his books provide a valuable source of social and linguistic history for the area, and we are indebted to him for that.

There is still much work to be done on W. G. Lyttle. In the course of preparing this introductory piece other snippets of information about the man and his writing came to the fore, but as they lead off on tangents that would require deeper investigation they were considered beyond the scope of this essay. Its purpose, as stated earlier, is only to draw a quick vignette with a view to stimulating further research.

In conclusion, it would be remiss not to thank Kenneth Robinson, Mark Thompson and Dr. Philip Robinson who all kindly contributed to this introduction.

Derek Rowlinson,

Bangor, *January*, 2015

NOTES

1 *The Adventures of Paddy M'Quillan*, *The Adventures of Robert Gordon*, *Life in Ballycuddy* (*Robin's Readings*), *Sons of the Sod*, *Betsy Gray*, and *Daft Eddie*.

2 Lyttle's house stood at the corner of Clifton Road and the Ballyholme Road. It was demolished by the Department of Environment on Saturday 13 March 1982 to make way for a car park. In January 2015, Mrs. Dorothy Malcolm (*née* Adair), who lived on the Stanley Road in Bangor until 1954, proffered the information that the house faced on to the Ballyholme Road (it was, in fact, No.1 Ballyholme Road) and the gable wall and garden adjoined the Clifton Road. She remembers it as being a tall building, three storeys high, with the house name *Mount Herald* displayed above the front door. In her childhood it was owned by a builder called Savage whose daughter Betty taught at Trinity School on the Brunswick Road. Savage had another daughter, Jean, and a son.

3 This is located immediately to the right as one enters the gates to Bangor Abbey.

4 According to Stephen J. Brown in *A Readers' Guide to Irish Fiction* (1910) it was first published as *The Smugglers of Strangford Lough*, c. 1890, but Loeber in *A Guide to Irish Fiction 1650-1900* was unable to locate a copy to confirm this.

5 See *An Index to the Newtownards Chronicle 1873-1900 and the Newtownards Independent 1871-1873* compiled by Kenneth Robinson and published by the South Eastern Education and Library Board Library and Information Service (1990).

PUBLISHER'S NOTE

The text in this book has been taken from a file kindly supplied by the author's great-grandson, A. G. Lyttle, which was based on the R. Carswell, Belfast, edition of 1914. Some obvious typographical errors in the latter have been corrected and a few spelling alterations made for the sake of consistency. Several additional footnotes have been added and these have been indicated as editor's notes. In one instance, it appears that a sentence in the 1914 version is incomplete, but no previous edition was available against which to check it.

CONTENTS

DAFT EDDIE

OR

The SMUGGLERS of STRANGFORD LOUGH

Chapter I

IN the quaint old churchyard of Tullynakill, which overlooks the western side of Strangford Lough, there stands to this day a plain, grey granite slab. It is situated in an out-of-the-way corner of this ancient burying place, and so obscured as really to escape observation. To the casual wanderer amongst the tombs and over the mouldering bodies of the generations who have gone to rest, that damp, dark, grey, granite tombstone fails to attract attention. Should the wanderer chance to pause in front of it, he will read thereon no lengthened record of the life wiped out so many long, long years; no history of him whose ashes now mingle with their kindred dust. There is an inscription upon the stone, but into it the effacing hand of time has made many a blur and blotch. Date there is none—one word only is traced upon it in loving memory of the dead and that word is the name:

EDDIE.

The careless reader passes on. The observant reader pauses and ponders. Eddie! How strange! Who and what was he! Perhaps a curious history lies buried here!

Yes, reader, it is so. Come with me, and I shall unveil the mystery. Listen to me, and I shall tell you a true and wondrous tale.

. . . .

Nearly a hundred years ago Strangford Lough, then called Lough Cuan, was famous for its fish and oysters. So abundant was the yield and so great was the demand that but little time was devoted to agricultural pursuits in the district. A fleet of fishing craft sailed upon the now deserted waters, and the hardy bands of fishermen reaped a rich harvest from the blue waters of old Strangford. These men were not all natives of the country. There were amongst them dark-eyed, brown-bearded, fierce-visaged fellows, of rude speech, and still ruder manners, who hailed from other and warmer climes, but who had somehow found out this fertile spot; who fished in the same waters and lived in the same white-washed mud-built cottages as did the bold and honest lads of County Down. Judged by outward appearance, these men of foreign aspect lived the same lives and followed the same peaceful pursuits as their companions. Yet it was a subject of remark that, though less industrious, money was more plentiful with them. They spent that money freely, however, and the easy-going natives gave themselves but little concern regarding what had many a time excited curiosity and comment.

One of the men was looked upon as a leader in every project, as the Commodore of the Strangford fishing fleet. He was not a pleasant fellow—far from it. His physical proportions were those of a giant; his features were forbidding, nay, even repulsive; his manner was coarse, rude and bullying. Though most men somehow feared him, yet he had won a kind of respect for his undoubted courage; and he was admired for the freedom with which he spent his cash. And so it happened that daily intercourse made him familiar with the people of the district, who gradually forgot that he was an ill-visaged dog, and overlooked his coarse, ill-mannered bearing. And so it came also to pass that he was known by the complimentary title of "Commodore Bob."

The curtain rises upon the interior of a little cottage, nestling at the base of a sloping hill, and close upon the margin of Strangford

Lough. The brief course of an October Sunday has been run, and the sable wing of night spreads over sea and land. The picture presented outside the cottage is a cheerless one. The moon, in her last quarter, glints feebly, now and then, from amongst the dense masses of dark clouds sweeping heavily across the starless heavens. Big drops of rain fall at intervals from those clouds, like the precursors of an impending torrent. The wind-lashed waters of the lough roar hoarsely, and the fir trees upon the hill behind the cottage toss their branches wildly in the storm's embrace.

Let us peep within.

A bright turf fire blazes upon the hearth and in its cheery glare no candle is required. The surroundings, over which the firelight flits, so far as furniture and home comforts go, are of the humblest kind. An old-fashioned dresser, with but a scant display of coarse delph; a rudely-constructed settle-bed; a few rope-bottomed chairs; three or four home-made stools, and a rickety table completed the furniture. In one corner, convenient to the hearth, there is a heap of turf, dried branches of trees, and a pile of whins; in another corner stands some home-made cooking utensils—to wit, iron pots, pans, and griddle; a tea-kettle, and a big barrel for the holding of oatmeal.

The cottage is the abode of Willie Douglas, a decent, honest, hardy young fellow, half farmer, half fisherman: an easy-going, good-natured son of the sod, without an enemy in all the broad county, and whose heart is devoted to his young wife Maggie, and their first-born child—Wee Wully.

There is a visitor at the cottage to-night: a visitor who is unwelcome to one, at least, of the inmates. Commodore Bob had dropped in an hour ago and had ever since sat by the fire conversing with Douglas, but paying no heed to the young wife who sat at some distance from the hearth nursing her baby boy. He knew that he was not a favourite with Mrs. Douglas. Anyone could have read that fact in Maggie's eyes, as she sat with pale and troubled face glancing from one to the other of the two men, and eagerly drinking in every word that fell from the Commodore's lips. That worthy's face was more sinister tonight than usual. He appeared gloomy; smoked his pipe absently; stared steadily at the burning turf, and conversed only by fits and starts. Close by his side sat Willie Douglas. He smoked a black clay pipe; and, leaning forward, traced in the peat ashes, by means of an old pair of tongs which he held in his hand, odd devices. He did not aim at design, apparently—his movements were mechanical.

Suddenly he started from the reverie into which he had fallen, aroused by the gruff voice of the Commodore, who exclaimed:

"What's that, lad? What's that you're made in the ashes?"

"A'm jest lookin' at it, Bob; jest tryin' tae fin' oot what it is, but A canna mak heid or tail o't," replied Douglas, as he resumed his scrutiny of the tracing.

"What wuz ye tryin'? Wuz ye *tryin'* to mak ocht?" queried Bob.

The Commodore spoke the broad County Down dialect almost as well as the natives. Years of close companionship and daily intercourse with the people had led him to adopt their speech, manner and habits.

Douglas laughed. "Ay," he answered; "A wuz tryin' tae dra' an oyster, but if it's like ocht ava it's a turmot (turnip). Cum here, Maggie, what dae you mak o't?"

The young wife bent over her husband's shoulder, her hand pressing it with a gentle caress.

"A think it is like a turmot, Wullie," she said, smiling at her husband's attempt at drawing.

The Commodore bent his head nearer, and closely scrutinised the outline. As he did so, the scowl upon his features deepened. For fully a minute he remained bent over it; then, suddenly rising, he exclaimed:

"It's mair like a skull!"

"A skull!" cried the wife, alarm spreading upon her face; "a skull! Oh, Wullie, dear, what's gaun tae happen?"

Douglas made no answer. Like most men of his class he was grossly superstitious, and this evil omen excited in his mind the most horrible and unspeakable fancies. Unwilling to add to the evident terror of his pale-faced wife, he threw down the iron tongs, leaned back in his rickety chair, and forced a laugh.

"Blethers!" he exclaimed. "Haud your tongue, Commodore; yer aye sayin' somethin' tae scaur the weemin."

Then, turning round, he laid one hand tenderly upon the head of his sleeping child; with the other he patted his wife's white cheek. He would have spoken—said something, doubtless, to remove her rousing fears—but the Commodore interrupted with:

"Dae ye hear the wun'? There'll be a herricane afore mornin' or A'm mistaken. Whaur's yer boat, Wullie?"

"Heth, A had forgot!" cried Douglas, starting to his feet. "She's in the Kroobin' Hole, an' gin there's a big sea the sherp stanes 'il mak sair wark o' her bottom."

"Cum awa, an' A'll gie ye a han' tae draw her up the beach," said the Commodore. And, as he spoke, Douglas buttoned up his coat and lifted his hat from the floor, on which it had been lying.

As he did so his eyes met those of his wife. There was a pleading look in them which said, as plainly as speech could: "Don't go, Wullie!"

Douglas understood, and respected his wife's desire.

"The boat 'll mebbe tak nae herm," he said, addressing Bob.

But the Commodore's eyes could speak, also, and Douglas knew their language. They said: "Come," and Douglas dare not refuse to comply.

"A'll no be lang, Maggie," he said, turning to his wife. Once again he caressed his child's head with a gentle touch of his big horny hand, and once again he patted his wife's pale cheek—now wet with a falling tear. Then he turned to go.

At this instant a fierce-looking terrier, of great size, sprang from a corner where it had been lying, and, uttering an angry growl, seemed about to seize the Commodore's leg.

With a loud oath, Bob kicked savagely at the dog, and the animal, at a word from Douglas, went back to its corner, snarling viciously.

"Damn yer dug! What ails it at me?" growled Bob.

Douglas made no reply.

"We'll need a licht, mebbe," observed the Commodore; and, as he spoke, he drew something from a side pocket of his huge overcoat.

It was a dark lantern. Taking a red peat coal from the fire, he lighted his lantern, and carefully drew the slide.

A moment later and the two men, alike to all appearance in habits and pursuits, but, ah, how different in the eye of Him who reads the heart, had stepped out into the dark and stormy night.

As the door closed behind them, Mrs. Douglas bent over the drawing in the ashes. She had never seen a skull; she had never even been shown the ghastly outlines of one in a picture, and so could neither confirm nor dispute the statement made by the Commodore. But her heart, that monitor whose promptings are beyond mortal ken, warned her of approaching danger. With her foot, she obliterated the drawing; and then, as the tears fast filled her large eyes, she pressed the sleeping babe to her bosom, and murmured:

"Oh, dear! Oh, dear! This is afore sumthin' awfu'! There can be nae luck, nae blissin' aboot the hoose that Commodore Bob comes intil!"

And then she sat down by the fire. Sat down to wait for the return of her husband, to count the leaden moments, the weary hours; to listen to the fierce shrieking of the winds, and the sullen surging of the waters in their rocky bed.

....

Hardy by nature as the two men were, they felt constrained to turn up the collar of their rough jackets. The change of temperature from the cheery kitchen to the black shore was sufficiently sharp and sudden to take a man's breath away from him. It was not, therefore, until some minutes had elapsed that conversation opened, and even then the sentences were brief and disjointed.

A walk of a hundred yards or so brought Douglas and the Commodore to what was known as "the Kroobin's Hole," a small rock-bound cove where, in moderate weather the *Betsy Jane*—a stout fishing-boat owned by Douglas—lay moored. The place was dangerous in rough weather and during the "spring tides," at which time the *Betsy Jane* was hauled up into safer quarters upon a grassy bank.

The beaching of the boat was a matter involving some trouble and requiring some care. Half an hour had elapsed before the job was accomplished, and then the Commodore, lifting his lantern, turned to Douglas with the words:

"Ir ye reddy?"

"Ay," was the brief response; and the two worthies turning their backs towards the Kroobin Hole, and with Strangford upon their right, started forward at a steady swinging pace.

"Hae we far tae gang?"

It was Douglas who spoke.

"No very far," was the vague answer, and silence followed.

There was evidently a pre-arranged plan, mutually understood.

And such was the case.

For months past the Commodore and Douglas had been frequently together. Very often, too, they might have been observed in quiet, earnest conversation. The Commodore had urged Douglas upon a certain point; pressed him to take a certain step. He yielded at length; yielded unwillingly. Not for his own sake had he consented to the proposals of the Commodore but the prospect of bringing plenty—nay, possibly wealth—to his darling wife and child had ultimately decided him. And to-night Douglas was to be put to the test; a test before which many a stout heart quailed.

There was an ordeal to be passed through, a mystery to be unravelled, and Douglas felt strangely nervous and excited now that the ordeal was at hand.

What was it?

We shall see.

CHAPTER II

Nick Donnan's House

BIG drops of rain were falling thickly as Commodore Bob and Douglas silently pursued their dark and lonely way. They were moving slowly and cautiously now, for the path they trod was narrow, tortuous, and rugged.

Having reached a certain point, the two men struck off into a bypath, which, after numerous windings, led to a pile of old and ruinous buildings.

The place had once been the homestead of a wealthy bachelor farmer, upon whom evil days had ultimately fallen. One morning the farmer had been found dead, slain by his own hand, said some; while others gravely shook their heads, spoke of his hidden wealth amassed by smuggling, and whispered the ominous word—"murder!"

That was years before this story opens, and no one had ever tenanted the house since the memorable day on which the dead body of Nicholas Donnan had been found.

The spot was a lonely one, far from any human abode, surrounded by trees, and nearly a mile from any public road. Late wayfarers, passing it as they crossed the country for a "near cut," had spoken frequently of flitting lights and weird forms seen moving to and fro; and at the period of which we now write, the place was shunned by even the boldest of the natives, the belief prevailing, and universally, too, that Donnan's house was haunted.

Beyond all doubt it was the refuge of the owl and the bat. Nor could it be denied that often, at the midnight hour, unearthly screams and horrible noises issued from the ruined pile; while not a few stout-hearted fellows were to be found who told blood-curdling tales of the sights and scenes witnessed in Donnan's old plantation.

Of a surety the place was an uncanny one!

Towards this ill-omened spot the two men bent their steps, pausing ever and anon to listen, as though for some expected sound or signal.

The path seemed a familiar one to the Commodore, for he forged steadily ahead, guided by the faint ray of light which gleamed from his lantern. It was different with Douglas, who stumbled and hesitated, and in whose heart there was a feeling of superstitious awe and dread as he followed in the wake of his more courageous companion.

There was another figure upon the path that night; a weird-looking, agile figure, that glided along with stealthy, cat-like tread, some distance behind the two men, stopping when they stopped, and darting behind a tree or boulder as if in fear that the lantern's ray might be turned upon it and disclose its presence,

On reaching the deserted homestead, the Commodore passed through what had evidently been a doorway and, turning the light of his lantern full on, cast a glance of keen scrutiny around the walls.

Then he advanced to a big, square slab which had been the hearthstone, and, kneeling down near to it, knocked sharply three times with a pebble which he had taken from his pocket.

There followed a brief space of silence, during which the Commodore once more darkened his lantern.

Just at that moment a low chuckling sound was heard at one of the broken windows.

Douglas started.

"What's that?" he gasped, as he grasped Commodore Bob's arm.

The Commodore laughed softly.

"It'll be yin o' them vampires," he said; "there's a lot o' them aboot this auld hoose. Or, for that part, it might be Nick Donnan's ghaist."

A creeping sensation crept over Douglas, and his teeth slightly chattered. He was a superstitious being; and the dread of being thought a coward alone deterred him of instant flight.

Had the Commodore flashed his bull's eye in the direction of the window from whence the sound which startled Douglas proceeded, he might himself have felt somewhat uncomfortable.

He did not do so, however, but repeated his signal upon the hearthstone instead.

Another space of deathly stillness, and then a faint sound was heard—tap, tap, tap—the echo, as it seemed, of the Commodore's signal coming from *beneath* the hearthstone.

As the sound died away, Commodore Bob turned on his light, and with the pebble which he still held in his hand gave six distinct knocks upon the stone. Then he stood up and waited.

Douglas meantime preserved absolute silence, wondering what was about to follow, and vainly endeavouring to banish that creeping sensation which had taken complete possession of his frame.

Surprises were in store for him.

A low rumbling noise was heard underground; the floor trembled and shook as if agitated by an approaching earthquake; and the next moment Douglas felt a rush of hot air streaming upwards upon his face.

The hasty exclamation which he was about to utter was arrested upon his lips as he beheld the hearthstone slowly descending, leaving a huge chasm dimly visible in the yellow glimmer of the lantern's rays.

Then the rumbling, grinding noise ceased, one end of a ladder was suddenly thrust up through the gaping hearth, and then the Commodore spoke.

"Douglas," he whispered, "dinna speak, but just follow me."

So saying, he crept noiselessly down the ladder, and his companion prepared to follow. As Douglas placed his foot upon the first rung of the ladder he heard a voice from the surrounding darkness distinctly whisper:

"Wully Douglas, dinnae gang doon there!"

Bewildered and alarmed, Douglas paused, uncertain how to act. The voice of the Commodore, harsh and commanding, although subdued, decided him. It said:

"Cum doon, quick!"

Douglas obeyed, trembling in every limb, and firmly believing that Donnan's ghost had whispered him a warning. As he set foot upon solid ground, the Commodore caught his arm, and pulled him to one side. Then that odd rumbling noise was again heard, as the huge stone, worked by some unseen mechanism, swung slowly up into its accustomed place.

In the dim light of the lantern, Douglas saw a narrow passage, but of its length he was unable to judge, nor did his comrade allow him much time for calculation. Again taking Douglas by the arm, the Commodore simply said: "This way!" and led him forward.

They advanced some twenty paces, turned sharply to the right, and stood still.

Then the weird cry of a curlew broke the silence, and seemed to be re-echoed in the far distance.

But the Commodore was the curlew which uttered that weird cry.

A huge slab of stone turned, as upon a pivot; a flash of light and a rush of hot air blinded the now thoroughly alarmed Douglas, who was seized by at least half a dozen men, and dragged suddenly forward into a scene of revelry and carouse.

CHAPTER III

"The Merry Hearts"

IT was some time before Douglas could accustom his eyes to the blinding light, or bring his senses to bear upon the unexpected scene.

He was first conscious of being surrounded by familiar faces; of being grasped by friendly hands; of hearing salutations of well-known voices. His fears, therefore, at once took flight.

A boisterous shout of welcome had greeted his appearance; and then a very babel of voices saluted him in the set phrases of the day:

"Yer welcome, Wully!"

"Man, what wae ir ye?"

"Ye'll mak the grand Merry Heart!"

"Wur ye scaured, Wully?"

"Dinnae be yin bit feered, boy!"

And all the while loud peals of laughter echoed through the cavern.

"What'll ye drink, Wully?" said a big stout fellow, drawing the astonished Douglas towards a long table which was literally covered with bottles, jars, tumblers, and other drinking utensils.

"Ah, boys, there's some sense in that," said Douglas, able at last to find tongue, and anxious to show that he felt quite at ease.

And he soon did so.

A fluid in the tumbler thrust into his hand quickly disappeared. It was brandy, pure and unadulterated: liquor such as Douglas had never before in his life tasted, and as the potent spirit mounted to his brain, he became oblivious to everything but the present, and felt angry with himself for the suspicions which he had entertained respecting Commodore Bob.

Then he began to survey his surroundings. The place in which he found himself, with such gay company, was entirely underground, the rough stones with which the apartment was built projecting, more or less, at very frequent intervals. The ceiling and floor were roughly boarded. A long coarse deal table extended down the centre of the room.

A huge fire blazed upon the stone hearth, flaring up the wide, gaping chimney, with a tremendous roar, the flue being so constructed as to unite itself with the chimney of a cottage some distance off, thus concealing all trace of light or smoke in the neighbourhood of Donnan's house.

Around the walls hung many strange contrivances, quaint devices, and curious instruments, the uses or objects of which were unknown to Douglas. Freely interspersed with these were guns, pistols of various makes and sizes, and heavy swords, chiefly of the cutlass pattern.

These details Douglas took in at a glance. But the table, and certain of its adornments, somewhat awed him. At each end stood a candlestick, the base of each being a human skull. Through the top of each skull a hole had been drilled, and into this was inserted a wooden cross which supported three candles. Ugly, forbidding-looking yellow dips they were, but they blazed and spurted with as much energy and zeal as though they were of ten times as much importance.

A strange thought flashed across Willie's brain as he looked at these gruesome candlesticks. His mind went back to the figure which he had traced in the turf ashes upon his own hearthstone, and a presentiment of coming evil crept into his heart.

His musing was of short duration. A sharp knock upon the table created an instant commotion in the room. Those who had been standing instantly returned to their seats, those who had not risen when Douglas entered settled down in their chairs and fixed their eyes watchfully upon the new-comer.

At the head of the table sat a burly, broad-shouldered,

brown-bearded man, whose face wore a look of fixed and sullen determination, and in whose eyes, now sternly fixed upon Willie Douglas, there was a fierce and wolfish gleam.

A second sharp knock, given, as Douglas now observed, with the butt of a huge horse-pistol, was followed by perfect silence.

A third knock, and Commodore Bob rose to his feet.

"Captain," he said, looking over towards and addressing the individual just described; "Captain, I have here, as promised, a new recruit, willing to join the 'Merry Hearts,' and ready to do such work as may be allotted to him."

The tone of voice, the accent, the language, were all so different from that to which Douglas had been accustomed that he winked at the Commodore and burst into a fit of laughter.

"Silence!" shouted the Captain, in an angry voice, again striking the table fiercely with the pistol, which he still held in his hand.

Douglas was now thoroughly startled. He saw that every eye was steadily fixed upon him; he felt that something was about to happen in which he was to take a prominent part, and there came upon him, for the third time that night, that peculiar, undefined sensation which warns certain natures of approaching danger or impending evil.

The Captain stood up, and Douglas, in response to a sign from the Commodore, also rose from the seat he had been occupying. Involuntarily he fixed his eyes upon the Captain, feeling that he was about to be addressed by him. Something in the man's features appeared familiar to Douglas, but when or under what circumstances they had met he could not then call to mind.

"Douglas," said the Captain, in harsh, guttural tones, "I have heard good reports of you, and we are here to-night to make you one of us. You have already heard of our society by name. Listen, now, and I shall tell you some of its objects. Briefly stated, they are:

"First—The forming of a bond of union amongst our members.

"Second—The bettering of our physical condition by embracing opportunities sought for, and following plans laid down by our Captain and officers.

"Third—The sacrifice, when necessary, of all treasure, possessed or acquired, for the good of our cause. Later on you will learn more. Are you ready and willing to join?"

"A see naethin' wrang in ocht ye say," replied Douglas. "What dae ye want me tae dae?"

"To take the oath," said the Captain.

"What is it like?" asked the simple-hearted fellow. At a sign from the Captain, every man stood up.

When silence had been obtained, the Captain spoke, delivering the oath in short, abrupt passages, so that Douglas could, without difficulty, repeat it after him. But the oath, and the awful ceremonies attending it, must be reserved for another chapter.

CHAPTER IV

The Oath of Allegiance

DOUGLAS heard the words of the oath, but he did not comprehend their full meaning. He repeated the sentences, in obedience to the Captain's orders; but he did so mechanically, and scarcely knowing that he did it.

The oath was this:

> *"I, William Douglas, of my own free will and accord, hereby swear, vow and declare that I will keep secret the doings of the 'Merry Hearts of Down,' and that I will obey all orders given to me by my superiors. If I violate this my oath in any particular, I promise to die by my own hand should I escape the vengeance of the Society."*

At the very instant that the last words passed his lips, Douglas was seized upon from behind, his eyes bandaged, and his arms pinioned. Then, while still held firmly by either arm, a voice—the lips of the speaker touching his ear—said:

"Forward!"

Impelled by those who held him, Douglas advanced slowly, the only sounds which broke the now solemn silence being the tramp, tramp, tramp of many feet.

How far he walked he could not tell; there were pauses, and turnings, marches and counter-marches; and then he felt himself forced suddenly down upon his knees. The next moment his arms were freed from the grasp of the hands which held them; the rope which had pinioned him was loosened; his hands were set free, and the bandage snatched from his eyes.

The poor fellow was by this time completely dazed, and the

sight which met his gaze was one not calculated either to restore his scattered senses or to arouse his failing courage.

The apartment in which he found himself was certainly not that to which he had first been introduced. It was smaller, and black, entirely black—ceiling, walls and floor. There was light enough, though, for a very blaze of light almost blinded him after the darkness through which he had just passed.

As his eyes gradually became accustomed to the blinding light, the scene revealed to him filled his very soul with unspeakable terrors. The place was full of men—masked men, every one of them. At either side of Douglas stood one of them, each holding a long-bladed knife, the points turned towards his breast. In front of him was a table, black also, round which, sat thirteen men, all of whom wore black masks, and black cloaks with a red heart-shaped patch upon the breast. In the right hand of every man gleamed the blade of a heavy naked cutlass.

For the space of fully five minutes not a word was spoken. Not a sound broke the oppressive stillness save the deep breathing of the men and the sputtering of the thick tallow candles. The interval was doubtless meant to add to the impressiveness of the scene. Then, the central figure at the table, the one directly facing Douglas, stood up.

"Douglas," he said—and Douglas instantly recognised the Captain's voice—"you have taken the oath; now we shall test you. Remember, the moment you violate that oath you are a doomed man. Your death sentence has already been passed. Stand up!"

Assisted by those who kept guard over him, Douglas rose to his feet.

The Captain made a sign.

Then, with startling suddenness, the men who stood on either side of Douglas gripped him by the collar and adroitly stripped him of his coat. Next, the man upon his left tucked up the left sleeve of his shirt—right to the shoulder.

"Advance!" said the Captain.

In obedience to a gentle push from his guards, Douglas stepped forward to the table.

The Captain laid down his sword, and lifting a dagger, handed it to Douglas, with the brief command:

"Cut your arm!"

Willie was by this time absolutely speechless with wonder, and stood silently gaping at the grim, masked visage which confronted him.

In a low but distinct whisper, his right-hand guard prompted him:

"Jag yer arm," he said.

With trembling hand Douglas took hold of the dagger. His heart beat audibly as he placed the point of the weapon upon his bared arm, and pressed the hilt until a tiny red stream spurted forth.

One of the band, rising from his seat, produced from some hidden nook a bottle of wine and a ghastly-looking bleached human skull. Filling the skull with wine, he held it directly under Willie's bleeding arm, and caught in it a few drops of the crimson fluid. Handing the skull to Douglas, he said:

"Drink!"

Douglas, shudderingly, tasted the gruesome beverage.

The death-cup was next handed to the Captain, who tasted the contents, after which it was passed round, and every member partook of the blood-mixed wine.

Just as the skull was replaced upon the table, the cavern was shaken by a loud peal of thunder overhead. The heavens, long threatening, had at length burst forth. Rain fell as though a second deluge had come upon the earth; the lightning flashed and the thunder rumbled, forming a startling *finale* to the weird ceremony which had just been performed.

Once more the bandage was deftly placed upon Willie's eyes; his dress rearranged; again there was marching, and counter-marching; then a loud, ringing cheer, the bandage was torn from off his eyes, and Willie again found himself in the larger cave which he had first seen, surrounded by laughing companions, who, amid jests and handshakings, welcomed him boisterously as one of

"THE MERRY HEARTS OF DOWN."

CHAPTER V

Put to the Test

EVERYONE present, the Captain included, shook hands with Douglas, who noticed that the grip was a peculiar one—a distinct, sharp pressure being given to his wrist.

This, as he afterwards learned, was the grip of the brotherhood.

A sharp knock upon the table, given by the Captain, terminated the fraternal greetings, and the men crowded to their seats round the table. Douglas was placed in a chair convenient to the Captain, and next to Commodore Bob.

"Now, boys, fill your glasses!"

The order came from the Captain, and was promptly obeyed. Amid general laughter and subdued conversation, bottles were passed around and glasses filled by hands that were not niggardly.

"A toast!" cried the Captain.

All stood up, glasses in hand.

"A toast," repeated the Captain. "I give you the health of our new brother, and may he prove to be a good man and true."

Douglas had risen with the others, but a look from the Commodore and a pluck of his jacket brought him to his seat, from which he gazed in bewilderment at the motley group who drained their glasses amid a perfect storm of cheers and cries of "Hip, hip, hurray!"

Again the glasses were filled, and this time Douglas was permitted to join in doing the toast honour.

The sentiment given was a popular one with the "Merry Hearts," judging from their enthusiasm. It was:

"Success to *Free Trade* and confusion to all Gaugers!"

"Douglas, what d'ye think of that stuff?" asked the Commodore, as he watched Willie draining his glass with evident relish.

"Maun, dear, it's grand," said Douglas. "Whaur div ye get it?"

The Commodore laughed as he replied:

"The gauger would like tae ken the same thing, but ye'll ken by-an'-by."

A succession of raps upon the table procured silence.

"To business," said the Captain. "Any reports?"

For a few moments no one spoke. Then a man whose features were unknown to Douglas stood up.

"Captain," he said, "a member has proved false to us."

"Ha!" cried the Captain. "Who?"

"Number 19."

"What has he done?"

"Communicated with the commander of a revenue cutter and given information regarding our business."

"What was his object?"

"Blood money."

"Has he been secured?"

"Yes, Captain."

"And where is he now?"

"In the dungeon."

"Fetch him here."

"Yes, captain."

The man with whom the Captain had carried on the above dialogue made a sign to three of the company, who instantly rose and proceeded with him towards one end of the cavern.

"What's the meanin' o' this?" whispered Douglas to the Commodore.

"Wait a minute an' ye'll see," was the whispered reply.

Douglas keenly watched the movements of the four men. They placed their hands against the wall and appeared to push against it with all their might.

As they did so, a portion of the wall, about the size of an ordinary door, turned upon a pivot.

Beyond the opening all was darkness.

"Number 19!" cried a voice.

In response to the call, a man stepped out from the darkness into the light. As he did so, two of the four men laid hold of him and led him to the foot of the table, facing the captain.

Douglas recognised him instantly as a man named Magilton, who lived near Millisle. The fellow wore an air of defiance, and regarded the Captain with dark and scowling looks. He tried at the same time to shake off the hands of his guards, but they held him with a vice-like grip.

"The proof!" demanded the Captain.

Commodore Bob rose.

"Captain," he said, "two days ago a revenue cutter was sighted, lying off Millisle, and making signals. Number 19 had been suspected and was under watch. He was seen to put off in his boat at a point close to Templepatrick, and was taken on board the cutter, where he remained for upwards of an hour. Then he took to his boat again, sailed round by Copelands, and returned to Millisle at dusk."

"And the cutter?" queried the Captain.

"Stood out to sea, towards the Scottish coast."

"What have you got to say, Number 19?"

"Naethin'!" was the sullen reply.

"We'll make you speak, my man," was the Captain's answer.

As the Captain spoke he made a sign, which was evidently understood. The two men whose hands were not laid upon Magilton's person stepped to a corner of the cavern and lifted something that rattled and clanked out of a barrel which stood there.

They were chains: two stout, heavy chains. At one end of each was a ring, at the other end a broad iron band.

With a deftness that told of practice at the work the men swung the rings on to a couple of big hooks that were driven into the ceiling.

The chains were attached to instruments of torture—the thumbscrews!

Magilton was led directly beneath the dangling chains. He knew what was in store for him, and resisted with all his might. But in the grasp of four strong men he was powerless; and, in less time than is required to relate it, the iron bands were placed round his wrists, and the screws placed against his thumbs.

The unfortunate man now resigned himself to his fate, and stood glaring fiercely at his captors.

"Will you speak now?" said the Captain.

"No!" was the sullen answer.

The Captain made a motion with his hand, and the two men who held the screws turned them. The iron jaws pressed upon the smuggler's flesh. He bit his lip, but uttered no sound.

"Will you answer now?"

No reply, and again the men's hands were seen to move. A low groan succeeded, and then a scream, of:

"I will! I will! Let me go!"

The man was instantly released.

"Give me a drink," he gasped.

One of the attendants handed him a glass of brandy, which he swallowed with a gulp.

"Now, then," said the Captain, "tell us all?"

The man did not speak for several moments. Then he confessed that he had betrayed the society and given information to the Government in hope of a reward.

His confession was brief, but sufficient to startle his hearers and to excite a yell of execration.

"Kill him! Kill him!" was shouted on every side.

When the wild outburst of passion had subdued, the Captain rose to his feet. There was an instant hush as he stood up.

"Magilton," he said, "your own confession has confirmed the evidence of the witnesses against you, and you must die. No man can escape who breaks the oath which you have taken. Our rules provide that you may choose one of two deaths, the knife or the pistol, and also that you may slay yourself, or die by the hand of an executioner, chosen by the casting of lots. How do you wish to die—by knife or pistol?"

A minute of deathly stillness followed. Magilton's head hung forward upon his breast and he seemed to be communing with himself.

"Answer!" said the Captain.

"Pistol," replied the man, without lifting his head.

One of the four men instantly placed a pistol in Magilton's hand. He looked at it for a moment, turned it in his hands, partially cocked it, and then flung the weapon upon the ground.

"A'll niver kill myself!" he said.

"Then we must find you an executioner," said the Captain; "prepare to cast lots."

The Captain drew from a drawer at his end of the table a small canvas bag, containing something which, on being shaken, rattled like marbles. Looking at Douglas, he said:

"As you are a new member, I must explain what is about to take place. This bag contains pebbles, all of which are white, save one. That one is black. The members will all be blindfolded, the bag will be passed round, every member drawing out a stone until the bag is empty. The man who draws the black stone must act as the executioner of the culprit Magilton. Make ready!"

The men were supplied with black bandages, which they immediately proceeded to put round their heads, but that duty was performed for Douglas by Commodore Bob.

The bag passed round in silence, the only sound heard being the chinking of pebbles as hand after hand was thrust amongst them.

The chinking ceased.

The bag was empty!

"Unmask!" said the Captain.

The men tore off their bandages, and each held up his right hand.

"White," said the Captain, throwing down his pebble.

"White!" "White!" "White!" went round until it was Douglas's turn to speak.

But he sat speechless, a look of horror in his eyes, and his face white as the face of the dead.

He held in his hand a black pebble!

CHAPTER VI

A Fearful Ordeal

THAT fatal pebble, black and shining, that had once lain by the shores of Strangford and been washed by the shores of old Lough Cuan, seemed to possess over Willie Douglas the power attributed to the eye of the venomous and deadly rattlesnake. His eyes rested upon it with a fixed gaze of alarm; his lips moved, but from them utterance there was none.

The Captain was the first to speak.

"Douglas," he said, "fate has decided that you shall be early put to the test. It is your duty to carry out upon our former comrade the sentence of our band. The sentence is death. You have sworn to obey all orders given you by your superior officers. Your first duty is a trying one, and I hope you will not shrink from it. If you do, then two lives must be taken instead of one."

Then, turning to Commodore Bob, the Captain said:

"Make ready for the execution!"

It is doubtful if Douglas heard the words which had been addressed to him. If he did, certain it is that he failed to understand them. He made no sign, no movement; gave utterance to no word or sound.

There was a bustling noise in the cave—a shuffling and tramping of feet. Half-a-dozen men seized upon the hapless Magilton, pinioned his legs and arms with stout cord, and then tied him to a heavy iron staple which had been driven into the wall.

The man made no resistance, and spoke not a word. He held up his head bravely, and looked steadily in the faces of the men who bound him. Indeed, a smile, half amused, half defiant, played upon his lips as the knots were being tied which bound him hand and foot.

"Ready, Captain."

It was the Commodore's voice.

"Now, Douglas," said the Captain, in a commanding tone, "do your duty!"

But Douglas did not stir.

He merely turned his eyes from the black pebble to the dark face of the Captain. That was all.

The Captain waved his hand angrily; and, as he did so, Douglas was seized upon by several of the men and jerked rudely from his seat. The next moment he found himself standing face to face with the condemned man, a distance of about six feet separating the two.

At last he found tongue.

Battling with the terrible fear that had taken hold of him and utterly paralysed his whole being, he dashed aside the men who stood at either side of him, and, stepping boldly forward, close to the Captain, demanded:

"What am A to dae?"

"You are to take a pistol and fire at that scoundrel," was the cool reply. "If you miss your mark, or fail to kill him, you are to fire again, and again, until he is dead. Do you understand?"

"A dae!"

"Will you obey?"

"A'm d——d if A wull, for you or ony ither man!"

A shout of laughter from the men drowned the Captain's answer, and he was obliged to repeat it. He said:

"You *will* obey! At all events, we shall try to *make* you obey. If you prefer to die rather than to execute that villain, then die you shall, even though I must kill you with my own hands."

There was no doubt in Willie's mind now as to his position. Every word spoken by the Captain sounded like a death-knell in his ears. He felt that the Captain was quite capable of carrying out his threat. A fierce tumult raged within his heart, and in the space of a single moment of time his whole life seemed to pass, panorama-like, before his mental vision. But in all that picture nothing stood forth so visibly as the cottage at the foot of the hill, the fire slowly dying out upon the hearthstone, the sleeping child, and the anxious wife, waiting for her husband's return.

The vision nerved him.

Without another word he turned round, and, looking at the Commodore, simply said:

"Show me what A'm to dae."

The Commodore drew the heel of his boot across the floor, marking a line in front of the condemned man at a distance from him of about two paces.

"Stand there!" he said.

Douglas instantly toed the line.

The Commodore took down from the wall a heavy horse pistol and pushed the ramrod into the barrel.

It indicated the presence of a heavy charge.

Then he pulled back the hammer and examined the priming.

"Is it all right?" asked the Captain.

"Right it is, Captain," said Bob, and he handed the weapon to Douglas.

Poor fellow! His face was ashen, his hand shook, and the heaving of his breast told of his agony more eloquently than words.

And Magilton—what of him?

Was he the hardened wretch he seemed, or did he wish to have it said of him that he had died game. He actually laughed—a full, hearty, rollicking laugh it was, too, without a particle of nervousness about it.

"Ir ye nervis, Wullie?" he asked

Douglas did not answer. He was waiting for the word of command, and every moment seemed an age. He could not look at Magilton. In fact, he had determined not to look at him—he would shut his eyes and shoot at random.

The doomed man was apparently the most cool and collected

of all present. While a whispered conversation was being carried on by the Commodore with some of the other men, Magilton whistled one or two bars of *The Girl I left behind me.*

"Make ready!"

It was the Captain who spoke. He had risen to his feet, and at the word two men took up their positions, one on each side of Douglas. Each man held a pistol in his right hand.

"Douglas," said the Captain, "I have no wish to cause you pain or to prolong the sufferings of the condemned man. Just a word, however. You will be covered by the pistols of the men who stand beside you; and if, at the word 'Fire!' you fail, to obey the order, you yourself will be shot dead upon the spot."

All this had passed in much less time than is required for the narration of the tragic scene.

Douglas glanced to the right. There was a pistol levelled at his head, and almost touching his hair. He looked to the left. Another huge barrel pointed towards him there.

"Ready!"

Douglas, guided by the hand of the Commodore, raised his weapon to a level with his breast, pointing towards his victim. He closed his eyes, and waited.

"Fire!"

He pulled the trigger. A loud explosion echoed like thunder through the low-roofed cavern; a wild shriek blended with the noise; the smoking weapon dropped from Willie's hand, and he himself staggered forward and would have fallen had he not been caught by the strong arms of Commodore Bob.

CHAPTER VII

Daft Eddie

STRANGFORD Lough, known in bygone days as Lough Cuan, takes its present name from the small town of Strangford, which stands on the west side of the narrow entrance into it from the sea. It is related by ancient historians that the lough had its beginning from the sea bursting into and overwhelming this flat tract of country, A.M. 1995, in the time of Partholanus, 339 after the Flood, or Universal Deluge, according to the Hebrew calculation. Probably this is the lake mentioned under the name of Darnart in John de Curcey's* Foundation Charter of the Black Priory of St. Andrew in the Ardes, for, by the said charter, he endows "that house with ten with ten plowlands in the territory of Art (*i.e.*, the Ardes) in the hands of Mac-Colloqua (their ancient proprietor) and with all the tithes of his demesne from the water of Dar-na-art, to the water of Carlingford." Now, as Dar-na-art literally signifies *by* or *through* the *Ardes*, and as Lough Cuan (or Coin) is the boundary of the greater portion of the Ards to the west, it is not improbable that it is the same which was called Darnart in the said charter.

The extent of the Lough from Newtownards in the north to Strangford in the south, is about thirteen Irish miles. It has been computed to cover 25,755 acres, Irish plantation measure. In conformation it somewhat resembles Italy. Its breadth is three miles in some places, in others upwards of four miles, and the tide flows right to Newtownards.

It is a prevalent saying that Strangford Lough contains an island for every day of the year—365. Whether this be true or not, the water certainly abounds with islands, some of which are

* Sir John de Courcy was an Anglo-Norman knight who played a prominent role in the conquest of Ireland during the 12th Century.

of considerable extent, and very many of which have had names bestowed on them.

The largest of these is Mahee Island, which contains fully 100 acres, and upon which at present a well-known farmer resides.

There lived upon Mahee Island, at the period of our story, Robert and Lizzie Barbour, man and wife. They were childless, and Mrs. Barbour, like most of her sex pined for offspring, and murmured against Providence which had made her barren. She prayed for a child—and one came. Not in the ordinary way, however, but in a much more romantic fashion.

One evening, as Mrs. Barbour watched by the shore for the return of her husband, who had been out fishing, a strange craft came in sight, steering right where she stood. In a few minutes the sails were lowered and the keel of the boat grated upon the shingle of the beach.

There were two persons on board—the boatman and a woman. The former, leaping out, stood with the water almost to his knees, and, taking from the woman a bundle which she carried, placed it tenderly in Mrs. Barbour's arms.

The bundle contained a living child.

Mrs. Barbour looked from the child to the boat, saying nothing until her visitor should land. To her surprise, however, the man—doubtless acting upon instructions—pushed the boat into deep water, clambered on board, brought round her bows towards the opposite shore, hoisted his mainsail, which speedily filled, and was off like a bird upon the water before Mrs. Barbour fully realised what had actually taken place.

A feeble cry from the animated bundle appealed to her womanly heart; and without giving further attention to her mysterious visitor, Mrs. Barbour hastened back to her cottage, which was not far off. Here she unwrapped the wrappings of the little stranger, and in a very few minutes was discharging the duties of a nurse as naturally as though she had been trained to that office.

Later on her husband arrived, and stood with gaping mouth while she related what had happened. Like good, kindly people as they were, no time was lost in coming to a conclusion. The child should be kept as though it were their very own. If its parents or friends came to look for it, or to explain why they had so unexpectedly bestowed it upon a childless woman, well and good. If no one came to look after it, why, well and good again. So long as it lived, or they were spared, it should have the bit and the sup, a roof to cover it, and the tender care of two honest, worthy people.

And so it was settled.

That night, when stripping the little stranger, a letter was found—and a big, fat letter it was. Mrs. Barbour, being the better scholar of the two, opened it, and forthwith a goodly bundle of banknotes dropped into her lap.

"Fifty poun', Robert!"

"Fifty poun', wuman!"

"Naethin' mair nor less; there, coont it yersel'." And in a fever of excitement the woman handed the banknotes to her husband.

He took them in his big, coarse hands, and looked at them as though he doubted their genuineness. Then he sat down and spread them out upon his knee; spat upon his thumb, and began to count, slowly and deliberately.

On finishing, he handed them back to his wife—who, by the way, was purse-bearer—and merely remarked:

"As true as daith!"

In their excitement, the letter was for a time forgotten. At length Mrs. Barbour bethought her of it; and, unfolding the sheet, began to read. The paper was thick and good; the writing bold and legible, but written evidently by a female hand.

The letter ran thus:

"Mrs. Barbour,

"You are no stranger to me. I know you well; therefore I entrust this child to your care. Call him Eddie; be good to him; love him as

though you were his mother. Make no enquiries, answer no questions, and you shall never know want. Spend the money which goes with this in any way you please. Twice in every year a good fairy will visit you and supply you with means to make Eddie comfortable. Good-bye."

The perusal of the letter required time, plainly written though it was, for the good woman to whom it was addressed had received but scanty schooling. She managed to spell it through, however, over and over again, until every word of it was fixed clearly in her mind, and then:

"A wunner wha's waen it is!" she exclaimed.

Her husband, a big, awkward man, slow of motion, but clear of head and warm of heart, laughed.

She turned upon him suddenly, with a look of anger in her eyes.

"What ir ye lauchin' at?" she snapped.

"At you," he said, quietly.

"What for, Rabert?"

Robert laid his broad hands upon his knees, and bending over the child looked at its little pale face long and earnestly. Then he said to his wife:

"Dizn't the letter tell ye tae ax nae questions an' tae answer nane?"

"It diz, Rabert; but then——"

"*But then,*" he retorted, laughing again; "yer jist like a' the rest o' the weemin, as fu' o' kureosity as an egg's fu' o' meat. Hain't ye noo got what ye wur aye wantin'?"

"What's that?" she asked, somewhat mollified.

"A waen," said Barbour.

It was now the wife's turn to laugh. She blushed, too, and bent over the infant to hide her confusion.

"Puir wee thing," she murmured; and then, as the child moaned in its sleep, she fondled it to her breast, and began to sing softly and soothingly, as only a woman can.

And so the child Eddie was duly installed under the roof-tree in Island Mahee. The choice of a foster mother had been wisely made.

....

"Whaur hae ye been the nicht, Eddie, ye senseless laddie? Doon by the shore, A'll warn ye, watchin' the waves, or efter some ither fool nonsense."

"Ay, indeed, mammy; an' A was farder than that tae; A wuz ower at the White Rock, spyin' farlies."*

"Ye'll spy a lock o' them afore ye mak muckle o' them. But, waen dear, yer clean drookit!"

"Weel, mammy, that's nae wunner; ye wudnae row a boat yersel' frae the White Rock a' nicht like that athoot gettin' wat. My! but the waves wur bonnie, wi' their white nichtcaps on them, dancin' and dancin' up agen the rocks, an' then splashin' back agen—"

"Pit aff yer claes this minit, ye idle chiel, or ye'll get yer daith o' cauld. Pit aff yer claes and get till yer bed. A nice jab A'll hae o' it dryin' yer duds in the mornin'!"

Well-nigh twenty years had passed since baby Eddie was borne across the waters to Island Mahee, and the conversation recorded above passed between him and his foster-mother. She spoke as though in anger, but, with Eddie she never could be annoyed. It was the manner of the woman, somewhat rough upon the exterior, but of warm, generous impulses, and kind, womanly heart.

From his infancy Eddie had been a spoiled and wayward child. Ignorant of his parentage, but believing him to be the natural son of a nobleman in the county, and being liberally paid for his support, the Barbours never asked, or even allowed, Eddie to do any work. His peculiar manner in early years earned for him the title of "the daft waen," and when he grew in years and stature to be no longer a "waen," he became known far and near as "Daft Eddie." His days

---

* *Spy farlies:* 'To pry about for any thing strange' – William Hugh Patterson's *Glossary of words in the Counties of Antrim and Down.*

were spent running over the island or sailing in his own little boat upon the bosom of Lough Cuan, exploring the islands, and paying frequent visits to the people who lived inland—with all of whom the guileless, chatty, engaging youth was an especial favourite.

Eddie's was one of those peculiar, ever-fitful natures of which most towns and villages have specimens—shrewd, intelligent by times, and keen in repartee, yet possessing many of the qualities of the half-witted child of Nature. In person he was tall and slender; sinewy and agile as a cat, yet in all his movements there was an appearance of awkwardness. In disposition he was exceedingly shy; so much so that, though having countless kind acquaintances, he had no confidants. Even with his supposed parents—Mr. and Mrs. Barbour—he was particularly shy and reserved; keeping his own counsel, yet doing exactly what pleased himself, appearing and disappearing at all sorts of odd times and places. Of reading he was passionately fond, and his mind, stored with old songs and ballads often ran wanton with poetical effusions.

From his earliest infancy, Eddie had been subject to sudden likes and dislikes, as is common with all people of a similarly constituted mind. Latterly he had shown a violent fancy for the child, Willie Douglas. With this little creature upon his back he would wander for hours by the seashore, the child and his queer nurse being often observed many miles from home. When questioned on these occasions he would make answer briefly and mysteriously, partly, perhaps, from a weak desire of appearing mysterious, and partly owing to his retiring disposition and his love of solitude.

And now, having thus fully introduced to the reader Daft Eddie, one who is destined to play an important part in this narrative, let us turn to other scenes and other characters already touched upon.

The reader is doubtless anxious to have another peep into the smuggler's cave under Nick Donnan's haunted house.

The reader shall be forthwith gratified.

CHAPTER VIII

Which is Partly Explanatory and Partly Anticipatory

THE shock sustained by Willie Douglas, when he fired the pistol at Magilton, was so severe that, strong man though he was, he swooned away, and did not recover consciousness for some time.

And now, as he lies in a dead faint, surrounded by a group of his companions who are endeavouring to restore him to his senses, the reader may be told that the execution was a sham one, the whole affair being a part of the ceremonies of the initiation practised by the "Merry Hearts," and designed to test the nerve and courage of the candidates who sought entrance to the gang.

The charge brought against Magilton was without foundation, the torture by the thumbscrews was an imaginary torture, the casting of lots was so arranged that the black pebble should fall to Douglas, the pistol was merely charged with powder and wadding. It must be added that Magilton had been carefully trained to his part of the farce, and that he played that part with all the naturalness which a professional actor could display upon the stage.

When Douglas opened his eyes, he stared wildly around him. Laughing faces were everywhere visible. It was some time, though, ere he could believe the evidence of his returning senses. He made no effort to rise, but lay wringing his hands, moaning piteously, and murmuring:

"A hae shot a man! A hae killed Magilton!"

Before long, however, under the potent influence of brandy and the good-natured chaffing of his companions, he was aroused, and soon became convinced of the real state of affairs. Magilton himself, alive and unhurt, wrung him by the hand and assured him that "it was a' but a joke." Commodore Bob explained the object the band had in view, and even the grim visage of the Captain relaxed into a smile as he assured Willie that his hands were free from the blood of a fellow being, and that, on the whole, he had acquitted himself like a good and brave man.

And then the liquor circulated freely; so freely that not a few of the men exceeded the bounds of moderation and became helplessly inebriated. The usual scenes followed. Some sang and shouted; others became sulky and wanted to fight; others, again, lay down upon the floor and fell into dreamless slumbers.

One of the latter was Douglas. The hour of midnight had passed before he was removed from the cave. The fresh air as he emerged from the stifling underground den partly sobered him, but for a time his limbs refused to support his tottering frame. Leaning heavily upon the supporting arms of two men, he ultimately reached home. His appearance caused his wife a severe shock, but she was a wise woman, and did not betray her vexation either by looks or words. Willie was assisted to bed, and slept soundly as though nothing had happened to disturb the ordinary uneventful tenor of his daily life. He slept the sleep of the drunken!

. . . .

As the sun rose from behind the mist-crowned hills of the fair Ards, Eddie was donning his clothes, which had been carefully dried before the fire. Having partaken of a hearty substantial breakfast, he left the house, launched his little boat, and pulled away towards the dwelling-place of Willie Douglas.

The night of storms was over. The sun had risen bright and beautiful; the sky was almost cloudless, and a gentle ripple upon the face of the blue waters was the only remnant of the wild surging of the billows on the previous night.

Presently the boat ran up on the beach. Eddie jumped ashore, hauled his craft into a place of safety, and then bounded into the cottage calling for his "wee Wullie."

The child heard the familiar voice, opened its bright blue eyes and crowed, and stretched out its arms towards its big, awkward playmate. Eddie lifted the little one tenderly in his arms, and, seating himself by the fire, opened a conversation with the infant—the greater part of which, need it be said, was carried on by himself. True, the child uttered sounds, but they were unintelligible, a circumstance which is but too frequently the case with persons of mature age.

"Ye'll be a richt nurse, but no a terble bonnie yin, when ye hae a waen o' yer ain," said Mrs. Douglas, after making sundry pantomimic gestures at her child. These gestures were of the kind familiar to mothers consisting in plunges made towards the infant as though she seriously meant to devour it alive, then starting short and, laughing vigorously. This was followed by murmurs of fondling endearment, audible amongst which were the words or phrases:

"Och, him's wee eysey pyseys; an' och, him's wee nosey posey!"

The child laughed too, evidently entering into the spirit of the fun, as it kicked and crowed in a manner that to a grown-up person must speedily have proved fatal.

"A waen o' my ain!" cried Eddie. "Shair this yin's my very ain! Irn't ye, dear? (This to the child.) Ir ye no jist Eddie's ain wee Wullie?"

And the baby crowed and laughed as though it quite understood and relished Eddie's joke.

And then Eddie, carried off by some odd flight of his fancy, sang, or rather chanted, the old song beginning with:

"Hame cam oor guid man at e'en,
An' hame cam he;
An' there he saw a man
Whaur a man shudna be.
'Hoo's this! noo, kimmer?
Hoo's this?' quo he—
'Hoo cum this carle here
Without the leave o' me?'"

"Is Willie gaun oot till the fishin' the nicht?" enquired Eddie, abruptly, after he had finished his song.

"If the weather's guid he's gaun ower tae the Kirkcubbin shore tae try his luck," said the woman.

"The say the fish ir a' lavin' this airt," remarked Daft Eddie.

"Ay, Eddie, so A hear them sayin', an' Wullie says he'll mebbe be oot a' nicht. A dinnae like sic lang fastin' an' sic lang cruises in weather sich as this."

"Why, Maggie?" queried the lad, innocently.

"Ah, Eddie, dear, the danger o' the water's bad eneuch, but there's waur nor that, A doot!"

"What wad it be, Maggie?"

"Them 'Merry Hearts,' Eddie. A'm tell't there's naethin' ower bad for them. A buddie cud forgie them for smugglin' a grain o' tay, or the like o' that, but A'm tell't they rob fowk's hooses, an' wha kens but they micht steal the very fish oot o' Wullie's boat, and tak his life intil the bargain."

"*You* neednae be feered o' the 'Merry Hearts,'" said Eddie. And then he paused, as though fearful that he had gone too far.

Mrs. Douglas noticed his confused looks; noted the abrupt manner in which he stopped, and her quick ear caught the emphasis placed upon the word *you*.

"What maks ye say that, Eddie?" she asked, a feeling of uneasiness stealing into her heart.

"Say what?" replied Daft Eddie, in a vacant, listless manner.

"Ye said *A* neednae be feered. What fur shud *A* no be feered ony mair nor ither fowk?"

"A dinna ken," was Eddie's answer, given in the same vacant fashion; and then he handed the child to its mother, with the remark:

"A'll no tak wee Wully wi' me the day, acause A'll mebbe be a guid while awa'."

With her child in her arms, Mrs. Douglas accompanied Daft

Eddie to the shore; saw him aboard, and stood watching him till his little boat was but a speck in the distance. Then she returned to her cottage, murmuring as she did so:

"Eddie's no as soft as some fowk tak him tae be; A wunner what he meent by what he said. There's sum devilment in the wun' A'll be boun'; but A hope ma Wullie haes naethin' tae dae wi' it. A wunner whaur he got the drink last nicht."

Meantime, Daft Eddie was also communing with himself, somewhat after the following fashion:

"So they're gaun the nicht, ir they? A didnae think they wad gang sae sune. An' Wullie's tae be wi' them, is he? An' he tell't Maggie they wur gaun tae Kirkcubbin, did he? He said he was gaun tae fish! My sang, but it'll be queer fish they'll be gruppin'. It'll tak me a' my time tae pit a stap tae this bizness!"

Eddie bent to his oars, and his swift craft shot over the blue waters like a feathered arrow.

His destination was Kirkcubbin; his mission thither shall be learned later on.

CHAPTER IX

The Smugglers

"STOLEN waters are sweet, and bread eaten in secret is pleasant."

So wrote Solomon, the son of David, the king of Israel—the wise man.

Of a truth, Solomon *was* a wise man—the wisest of all men!

Much of what he wrote and spake three thousand years ago holds good to-day. If he were living now he would probably say: "Smuggled brandy and tea are sweet, and tobacco smoked in secret is pleasant." And he would be right.

Yes, Solomon was a wise man, though he lived so long, so very long ago.

He understood human nature.

Our story does not date back three thousand years; no, not even three hundred; no, not nearly one hundred—and even so recently as that:

"Smuggled brandy and tea were sweet!"

So sweet were they that both men and women throughout Ireland, England and Scotland, risked their very lives to obtain them. And they are just as sweet, nay sweeter, at the present day. The greater the risk, the sweeter the reward. Smuggling is a more difficult thing nowadays than it was from fifty to a hundred years ago, but it goes on still, and will go on, even to the end of time.

And why shouldn't it?

The brave, hardy smuggler is a hero; admired even by the Government-paid creatures who earn a livelihood by hunting him, and who are as far beneath him in manhood as the bailiff is beneath the oppressed tenant whom he seeks to hunt from his home and country.

Long live the smuggler!

He does live; and he will live. The sleuth-hounds of the government may be on the watch; but they are men, and poor specimens at that; their wits may be keen and their cunning wondrous, but there are clearer heads and sharper wits to be found, and so the brave old game of smuggling goes on under the very noses and eyes of the government ferrets!

Human nature will be human nature still!

At the time of which we write, smuggling was in full swing. There were brave men in those days, men whose very daring made them noble in the eyes of the people against whom they lived. Dynamite was unheard of; revolvers and repeating rifles were unknown. Gunpowder and leaden bullets existed, though; bludgeons and knives were in abundance. The use of these was well understood: the value of them was duly appreciated.

In nearly every, if not every, maritime country there were known to be gangs of smugglers. France and Holland were not out of reach; the Isle of Man was a convenient go-between; brandies, wines, gin, tobaccos, cigars, teas, silks, and East India goods were as much relished then as they are now, and they were all the more highly appreciated if they reached the consumer or the wearer *duty free.*

Dues were high in those days, and the temptations to smuggling were strong—nay, even irresistible. The importation, too, of certain goods was prohibited by government, for which very reason these contraband goods commanded almost fabulous prices.

Adam and Eve live still! That which we are forbidden to partake of that do we hunger and thirst after!

The system of prevention is very more effective now than it was fifty years ago. The revenue men were treated with such undisguised contempt by the coast people that they naturally felt ashamed of their contemptible calling, and so on many occasions wilfully closed their eyes against what was going on under their very noses.

As far as Ireland was concerned, smuggling was carried on with the most open daring. Ulster was not a whit behind the other provinces; and, in the districts in which this story deals, the fascinating game of cheating(?) the government was engaged in by all classes. Nearly all the farming and lower classes were actively engaged in it, and the upper classes encouraged the practice by purchasing the smuggled goods. The fruits of smuggling remain in County Down up till the present day, and the writer could point to scores of homesteads, along the coast and Island, which have been reared and fattened by the hardy smugglers of a generation now extinct.

All round the County Down coast, caves used by the smugglers are still well known, though now unused. By the shorelands of Greypoint, Carnalea, Bangor Bay, Groomsport, Donaghadee, Millisle, Ballywalter, Ballyhalbert, Ballyferris, Cloughey, and right along to Ballyquintin Point, the smugglers had their caves; while amongst the islands and along the shores of Strangford Lough a perfect network of hiding places existed. Boats chased in the open sea by revenue cutters usually made for Strangford Lough, crossing the Strangford Bar without fear, even in stormy weather, and laughing at their pursuers, who dared not follow. Once safely past Portaferry all danger was, for the time, at an end, and the "cargo" was stowed away without difficulty.

With these caves, however, and the uses which were made of them in bygone days, we shall deal later on.

The reader will have already guessed that the "Merry Hearts" of Down were smugglers.

The reader has guessed correctly.

But the "Merry Hearts" were more than that. They were robbers and pirates.

Smuggling has such a charm about it as to merit countenance. Few people can regard it as a dishonest practice. But piracy by sea or land—who shall defend?

The "Merry Hearts" held the people under a species of terror, for they were known by their deeds. Everything in the line of pillage seemed to come in their way, from robbing a hen-coop to piracy upon the high seas. These remarks, however, do not apply to the entire band. There was an outer circle and an inner circle. The former followed fishing, farming, and smuggling; the latter embraced every chance of gain that might turn up, and their dealings were, in nearly every instance, concealed from the more innocent men.

For a year, or possibly longer, the Inner Circle of the "Merry Hearts" had had in view a bold scheme of robbery and violence. Their plans had been carefully matured, and the chosen members who were to take part in the exploit had been sworn to secrecy, in the most solemn and binding fashion. Everything was in readiness, and the men waited for but one thing—their Captain's word of command.

The Captain waited also for one thing—the proper time.

That time had come!

The time had come, and the men were ready—ready for a deed of daring which was to thrill with horror, fear and indignation the hearts of every dweller in Killinchy and the Ards.

CHAPTER X

In Which New Scenes and Characters are Introduced

THE village of Kirkcubbin is pleasantly situated upon the eastern shore of Strangford Lough, in the barony of Upper Ards, about eight Irish miles to the south-east of Newtownards. It lies almost directly opposite to Killinchy, from the shore of which may be distinctly seen the white houses of Kirkcubbin that stand near the water's edge.

At the time of our story, as now at the present day, fishing was vigorously carried on in Kirkcubbin waters; and then, as now, fishing boats arrived and departed without any interference in the way of either demanding or collecting dues from the owners.

In the townland of Ballyeasborough, which is not far from Kirkcubbin, there lived, at the period of which we write, a certain Mr. Thomas M'Fadden. He was a magistrate—a well-to-do man—rich, indeed, in this world's goods; of an easy-going disposition, happy and contented, if appearances were to be judged by; at peace with all men, honoured and esteemed by everyone who knew him.

He held broad acres of well-tilled and richly-cultured lands; his horses, cattle, and sheep were the best in all the wide peninsula of the Ards. His house, while not resplendent with the luxurious appointments which are the products of modern times, was comfortably and expensively furnished, every apartment presenting an aspect of cosiness, comfort, good cheer and hospitality.

Mr. M'Fadden was his own banker; he did a tolerably large business in the money-lending line amongst the Ards farmers; bought and sold horses and cattle on a large scale, and was known to have at all times a good store of yellow golden guineas ready for loan upon fair and reasonable security, or for investment or some speculation likely to prove profitable.

But the greatest treasure possessed by Mr. M'Fadden—at least in his eyes and estimation—was Martha M'Fadden, his only unmarried child, a bright, winsome, beautiful girl, who had cheered him in his years of widowhood, and whose presence was the very sunlight of his life and home. Her portrait, till this day, hangs upon the wall of a certain house in the Ards, painted after the style of artists of the olden days and it discloses a face of rare sweetness and surprising loveliness.

But of Martha more anon.

The "Merry Hearts of Down" had marked Oakville—the residence of Mr. M'Fadden—for robbery and pillage by their band. The name has been changed in latter days, but many readers of these columns will remember when the house and grounds were known by the title of "Oakville." The dwelling-house was long, low and angular; full of old nooks, rooms and corridors. The outer walls were covered with a rich trellis-work of roses which, in their seasons, blossomed up even over the broad thatched roof, and peeped in at almost every window, filling the place with a delightful fragrance.

The situation of Oakville was a charming one, occupying, as it did, one of the most pleasant and luxuriant spots in all the Ards.

The house stood at about the centre of the peninsula that stretches out towards the Irish Sea, commanding a fine view of the Belfast Lough; of the wild rocky headlands of the Antrim coast; of the Copeland Islands, with their variety of light and shadow, as they lie like twin children sleeping in a vast azure cradle; and of the nearer waters of old Lough Cuan, reposing in magic beauty amid bewitching loveliness of scenery.

Immediately at the rear of Oakville House were the yard and office-houses. Behind these, at a little distance, lay the orchard—a large and well-stocked one—while behind that again rose a gently-sloping hill. On either side of the house a fine wood extended for some distance, sheltering the farmhouse from the sharp blasts to which, from its position, it would otherwise have been exposed.

Upon this place, as has already been said, the "Merry Hearts" had fixed their attention, and a plot had been skilfully laid for robbing and pillaging the House of Oakville. Their plan, however, had been discovered by one whom of all others would never have been suspected by them. It was known to Daft Eddie, and the half-witted lad had determined to warn Mr. M'Fadden of what was about to happen; and, if possible, to defeat the robbers in their diabolical scheme.

We followed Daft Eddie from Island Mahee to the residence of William Douglas, and saw him embark thence for Kirkcubbin, where we shall now join him, on his mission, to warn the inmates of the house of Oakville, in order that they might take steps to protect their property and defend their lives.

As he approached the shore, he selected a retired spot for landing; and, drawing his light boat after him, concealed it in a thick plantation which grew down close almost to the water's edge. Shortly afterwards, Eddie's long, awkward figure made its appearance at the door of the village ale-house, at which establishment he was well-known and was at all times a right welcome visitor.

Public-houses were not so numerous in Kirkcubbin then as they are now. Robin Maxwell had all the trade to himself, and a fine, off-hand, honest, jovial fellow he was, as ever held an oar or quaffed a mug of beer.

Robin extended to Eddie a hearty welcome, and quickly provided for him a substantial meal, to which the hungry lad did speedy and ample justice.

Having satisfied the cravings of nature, Eddie started off upon foot for Oakville, where he arrived just as the shades of evening were beginning to fall.

He stood for a few minutes timidly surveying the quaint

old building, and then stepping up to the door he knocked for admittance.

As he did so, a sudden fear seized upon his heart. What if the "Merry Hearts" should discover him in what he was doing! What if, even now, some of their emissaries were watching his movements! What if some of the men servants about the place should turn out to be members of the gang! If Eddie were discovered in his efforts to betray the robbers, he would certainly be murdered by them. This thought had never occurred to him until the moment when he knocked, and then it flashed upon him suddenly and filled him with such overwhelming and unspeakable terror that he turned to flee from the spot.

But if he contemplated flight it was now too late. Ere he could make his first bound the door was opened, and a woman servant, with a hard face, but a still harder voice, asked:

"Wha ir *you*, an' what div ye want?"

CHAPTER XI

Evil Tidings

IN one of the cosy sitting-rooms of Oakville, on the night of Eddie's visit, sat Martha M'Fadden and Mrs Myrtlebrace, the English housekeeper.

A brief description has already been given of Martha, who has seen some twenty summers, and whose graceful figure, fine intellect, cultured mind, and ladylike bearing fitted her for a much more exalted sphere of life than that in which she now moved in Oakville.

But the lady who had come all the way from England to act as housekeeper for Mr. M'Fadden and his daughter, merits a word of introduction. She was of middle age and peculiar temperament; short, fat, fairly good-looking, melancholy. The cause of her melancholy was probably known but to herself. As a matter of course, people indulged in surmises upon the subject; but Mrs. Myrtlebrace, though somewhat communicative on other points, was silent regarding that one.

Some said—professing to have heard about it—that in early life the good woman had been crossed in love. Everybody agreed that her nervous system must, at some period of her life, have sustained a serious, if not a painful, shock. When pointedly questioned upon the subject, the lady generally heaved a deep sigh, and said she was afflicted with "a gathering at her heart." What this meant nobody knew; and enquiries, receiving but little encouragement, were seldom pushed further.

Mrs. Myrtlebrace was but seldom interfered with in her household duties, and was complete mistress of the situation. She was generally allowed to mind her own business, and she did mind it with a pertinacity that was highly commendable. What that business was, though, remained a profound secret to the generality of mankind—and womankind. From morn till night she bustled about through the old building, commanding and countermanding, doing and undoing, making things pretty lively and, now and then, unpleasant for the servants of the household, with whom she was far from being a favourite.

Upon the night in question Miss M'Fadden and the housekeeper sat, as has been said, in a cosy room.

Let us enter.

The fire burns cheerily in the capacious grate. The favourite cat lies curled up on the hearthrug. Miss M'Fadden reads. The housekeeper knits.

At length Martha, laying down her book upon the table which stood beside her, breaks a long silence, which has ensued, by yawning.

"Your book is not interesting, my dear," remarked housekeeper.

"Not particularly," was the young lady's reply.

"Ah, sure novels are never interesting," said the housekeeper; "and they're all a parcel of lies, too. In this sad and dreary world novels is awful tiresome."

Miss Myrtlebrace, though she had come all the way from England, did not speak the purest of English.

"Oh, surely you don't mean that?" exclaimed Martha.

"Indeed I do, my dear; I wouldn't read a novel, no, not if you were to—"

A smart tap at the parlour door prevented the completion of the sentence.

"Come in," said Martha, cheerily.

"Come in," echoed the housekeeper, despondingly.

"There's a boy at the daur, mem, that wants the maister," said the servant, popping in her head, and speaking generally to both the ladies.

"Let him wait till the master comes home," said the housekeeper, stiffly.

"Who is he?" inquired Martha, of the servant.

"A dinnae ken, Miss Martha."

"What is he like, Susan?"

"A very ornery lad, Miss Martha; but he says he maun see the maister at yince, for he haes cum a long wae, an' it's very important what he wants tae say till him."

"Take him to the kitchen, Susan, and let him wait there," said Mrs. Myrtlebrace, with a tone of decision.

"Yis, mem." And Susan closed the door.

But the girl returned in a few minutes, entering the room this time without knocking, and looking considerably excited.

"Well, Susan?" from both ladies.

"Mem, he says he maun see sumbuddy at yince! An A think ye had better cum an' speek till him, for he's terble raised lukin'."

The housekeeper rose, with as much dignity as her figure could assume, and followed Susan to the kitchen.

There she found Eddie, standing with his back to the fire, twirling his cap between his hands and looking wild and excited.

"What is it, boy?" she asked.

"Is the mester no here?" enquired Eddie, hurriedly, at the same time pulling his forelock deferentially.

"No, boy, he is not."

"Whaur is he? A maun see him at yince."

"You can't; you must wait. He has gone to Ballywalter."

Eddie twirled his cap vigorously. He had a confused idea that luck was against him; that his warning would be of no avail; that his long journey had been undertaken in vain.

Just then, drawn thither by a pardonable feeling of curiosity, Martha stepped into the kitchen.

Eddie's eyes instantly fastened upon her, and the girl's beauty fascinated him. So earnestly and fixedly did he gaze at her that the young girl flushed, and, turning away, addressed some enquiry to the maid, Susan. Directing that food should be given to the boy, and that he should be made as comfortable as possible, Martha went back to the parlour, closely followed by Mrs. Myrtlebrace.

Half an hour later, Mr. M'Fadden arrived from Ballywalter, where had he been transacting some business.

He was at once told that "a person" wanted to see him; giving directions that "the person" should be brought to him into his study, the worthy magistrate made his way down a long corridor, and into a neatly-furnished, old-fashioned room, which his daughter Martha had fitted up for him as a kind of office, or sanctum, in which he could receive his personal visitors, write his letters, and transact s his private business.

Throwing himself into a big arm-chair, and assuming an attitude of restful repose, he awaited the introduction of his visitor.

Let us look at him as he thus sits.

Of middle height, and somewhat stout in build, he apparently differed but little from the ordinary well-to-do farmer of the day. But the head and the face! A head beautifully formed, and covered with rich, wavy hair, silvery hair, and almost snowy white. A face bold, handsome, ruddy with the glow of health and animal spirits; teeth white as pearls, eyes blue as summer skies; lips red and laughing. Truly the man—and we paint him from life—was one man in a thousand.

As we sketch him, thus hurriedly, Eddie enters, and stands before him, shy, nervous, timid, twirling and tugging at his cap, waiting as though to have something said to him before he himself speaks.

He was unknown to Mr. M'Fadden, who surveyed him for a moment or so, and then said, in his wonted kindly tone of voice:

"You wish to see me?"

"Yes, your honner."

"You are a stranger in these parts, I think; may I ask your name?"

"Na, sur; A'd rether ye wudnae."

"Why, my lad?"

"It cud dae na guid if A did tell you, an' it micht dae muckle herm."

"Very well, my lad; sit down, take a chair."

But Eddie did not sit down. He advanced a step, and looking into Mr. M'Fadden's face, said in an earnest whisper.

"*It's a black business!*"

The magistrate smiled. He was accustomed to such observations from persons calling to consult him in his official capacity.

"And what is the business?" he asked, good-naturedly.

"*Hae ye iver heard tell o' the Merry Hearts, sur?*" said Eddie, very earnestly.

Again the magistrate smiled. Only too frequently had the reputation of these men reached his ears. Numerous villainous depredations had quite recently been perpetrated in his neighbourhood, but all efforts to trace the outlaws had failed. Now and then a schooner, bound to Kirkcubbin, Portaferry, Killeyleagh, or the other little ports that lie around the lough, had been attacked, boarded, and plundered. The mail coach to Belfast had been stopped and robbed several times; and, only a week previously, the robbers had scooped down upon a farmhouse, cows, and poultry.

"Yes, boy, I have heard of them. Well?"

"Weel, sur, A heerd a conversation the tither nicht at a meetin' o' some o' them boys that dinnae speek weel fur *you*, sur!"

"What was it, my boy?"

"Ye'll promise tae keep me safe, sur?"

"I will, indeed; now, tell me all you have to say."

And Eddie told him, speaking in short, jerky sentences; and every now and then looking over his shoulder towards the door, with a white scared face, as though fearful of being overheard by anyone hovering near.

Mr. M'Fadden watched the lad closely. He at once noticed the weak intellect, but there was that in Eddie's manner which convinced him to the truthfulness of his story.

And that story was a startling one.

At its close, the magistrate pondered for a few moments.

Then he asked sharply:

"Who are these men?"

"Eh?" said Eddie, vacantly.

"Who are these men? Tell me their names. You need not be a bit afraid."

"No, sur; A daurnae."

"Why?"

"They wad cut my throat!"

"I believe they would," said Mr. M'Fadden. "Very well, my poor boy, we'll let that pass. Tell me, at what time will they be here? Was there any hour fixed in your hearing?"

"A dae naw ken, sur. A heerd nae time named."

"No matter. Can you stay here all night?"

Eddie turned to go, with a wild look in his eyes.

"Na, sur," he cried, excitedly; "dinnae keep me. Mummy will wunner whaur A am a' this time that A hae been frae hame, an' if *they* ketched me here they wud cut my throat. A cum a lang road tae tell ye; an' God bless an' keep ye. Won't ye let me gaun awa noo, sur?"

"Certainly, my brave fellow; and I'll see you again to reward you for your courage. Here, take this."

He held out a piece of gold to the lad.

"Na, thank ye," said Eddie; "A hae mair money nor a need or ken what tae dae wi'. Mammy gies me plenty." And he turned to go, evidently impatient to be off.

Finding persuasion of no avail, Mr. M'Fadden conducted Eddie to the outer door, saw him out, and bade him goodnight.

Then he returned to his study; and, sitting down, endeavoured to decide upon a plan of action.

"I must tell them," he said; and, as he spoke, he rang a large hand-bell.

The servant answered immediately.

"Susan," tell Miss Martha and Mrs. Myrtlebrace that I wish to speak to them here at once. Be quick, now."

"Yis, sur."

The ladies were instantly on the spot.

Mr. M'Fadden, calmly and quietly, communicated to them the substance of what he had heard, and concluded by assuring them that they had nothing to fear.

"The house is fairly provided with arms," he said. "In fact, I could almost stand a siege by an army, so all you have to do is to obey such orders as I may feel called upon to give."

"And what must we do, father?" asked Martha, her cheeks pale, and her voice quivering; but still tried to look brave and unalarmed.

"I have that all arranged," said her father, who was perfectly cool and collected. "You shall both be taken to Robb's cottage. (This was a snug cottier house scarcely half a mile distant, the property of Mr. M'Fadden.) I will send you over by the car and in charge of two men who will stay with you as long as may be necessary. Leave the rest to me. There is no danger, remember that. The warning brought by this brave lad makes everything right, so you must promise me not to be alarmed or uneasy. I must stay here to receive these gentry. Now, be off! Take with you plenty of warm wraps, and I will have you back here before midnight—I hope."

Despite himself, his voice lacked its usual cheery tone. He knew, by repute, the desperate characters of the men with whom he had to deal. He was a man, however, of fearless nature and iron nerve—quick, energetic and resolute. Within half an hour the ladies were despatched to safer quarters, and then he instantly set about having his money, valuables, horses, and other live stock removed to Robb's cottage, where he felt certain nothing would be molested.

Having superintended all this as quietly as possible, so as not to needlessly attract the neighbourhood, he summoned his labourers around him. These were about four in number. They were brave, hardy fellows, though little versed in the use of arms. True, they could load a gun and fire it at a crow, a magpie, or a seagull, but their movements were slow and awkward. Mr. M'Fadden, however, felt that he could trust them to die, if necessary, at their post of duty.

And the men were ready to do so!

The house contained four guns—four old Queen Ann guns—no more! Rusty old weapons they were, too, and not to be depended upon for accuracy or powers of execution.

There was gunpowder in abundance; shot also, but bullets none. The men gathered nails and pebbles to act as substitutes.

Preparations, hasty as they were, occupied them till ten o'clock.

All was then ready for defence. The lights were then extinguished, and every man stood at the post assigned to him. The doors and windows had been barricaded with furniture and such other heavy articles as could be obtained.

Suddenly one of the men said:

"The dog, sur!"

"Yes, John. What about him!"

"Shud we bring him in, sur?"

"Indeed we should, John; I'll go for him myself. I'm glad you thought of that."

And Mr. M'Fadden went out for the animal, unwilling to expose his men to the possible danger of doing so.

But the dog was gone!

Clearly the "Merry Hearts" had their plans well arranged!

This was the second warning.

There was now no room for doubting. But one question remained: When would the robbers reach Oakville?

In black darkness, weary men, men tired with the day's heavy farm-work, and needing rest and sleep, stood with loaded guns in hands, waiting in anxious dread, listening with strained ears, for the ruffians who were to come, possibly with fire and sword, to destroy them.

Slowly the leaden moments crept on.

No sound but the men's laboured breathing, and the heavy, monotonous ticking of the big sombre eight-day clock that stood in the main corridor.

"Will they come at all?"

"Why don't they come at once!"

These questions were frequently asked in whispers.

Hark! What sound is that?

It is the cautious tread of heavy-booted men!

And, at the same instant, there is a sharp click, as M'Fadden raises the hammer of his ponderous gun.

Then he speaks—in a loud emphatic whisper:

"Ready, boys! Don't fire till you get the word from me."

CHAPTER XII

Besieged

MIDNIGHT had passed, and the, hour of one o'clock was approaching when the fatigued watchers in the barricaded house at Oakville heard the sounds described in our last chapter. The men were posted in different rooms, but all within hearing of each other's call, when given in a loud whisper.

The sounds of footsteps, moving cautiously round the house, was distinctly heard by them all.

The sounds ceased. Profound stillness. Deep darkness. The watchers with bated breath waited for what was to happen next.

Then, upon their straining ears came a peculiar noise, resembling the grating of a file upon iron or steel.

The sound proceeded from the direction of one of the back windows.

M'Fadden, taking one of his men with him, crept noiselessly into the room in which this rear window was situated. The night was somewhat clearer without than within the house, and M'Fadden, now thoroughly accustomed to the thick gloom within, was enabled quite plainly to discern the figure of a man outside the window, his right arm moving slowly backwards and forwards.

He was cutting through the sashes of the window with a small hand-saw.

M'Fadden observed fully a dozen men surrounding this fellow, and he also distinctly saw a number of others, like spectres, gliding about the yard and outhouse.

Doubtless they were watching for a light or other indication of the sleeping inmates having been disturbed or aroused, and were ready to give the signal of alarm to their comrades.

A closer inspection of the midnight marauders would have

disclosed the fact that all of them wore black masks upon their faces, and that their figures were so disguised as to render recognition impossible. Some had artificial humps upon their backs, and others wore long cloaks of peculiar and fantastic cut. Round the arm of every one was a narrow white band— the mystic badge or insignia of the order, by which they could recognise each other when engaged in business like the present.

M'Fadden felt that the time had come to act. The gun which he carried had been heavily charged with small shot—an act of humanity which he afterwards sorely regretted and bitterly repented.

Silently raising the gun to his shoulder, he took a hasty sort of general aim at the window and pulled the trigger.

The old Queen Anne clicked—blazed—banged, belching forth a terrific volley of flame, hail and smoke.

From the men at the window there burst a yell, loud and simultaneous. It was a yell of pain and terror, as the small shot, like red hot needles, penetrated the fleshy parts of their bodies. In a moment, however, they rallied, having discovered the comparatively harmless nature of the discharge, and a laugh was actually raised at one of the gang who had been standing with his back to the window, and who now, with his hands pressed tightly upon the region of his coat-tail, danced about the yard roaring like an infuriated bull.

By common consent a retreat was made towards the outhouses so that the nature and extent of the wounds might be ascertained, and M'Fadden began to solace himself with the belief that the robbers had taken flight, and to congratulate himself upon his easy and all but bloodless victory.

He was mistaken.

There was a loud shout from without; a rush of feet, a deafening crash, and the back windows of the house, were dashed into shivers.

"Fire!" cried M'Fadden. And his men, who had been standing in readiness, blazed away simultaneously.

Fatal mistake!

This was exactly what the "Merry Hearts" desired should take place. They had propelled heavy logs against the windows for the very purpose of inducing the defenders to discharge their weapons.

They had succeeded, and now, feeling that but little danger was to be anticipated, the freebooters boldly leaped in by the embrasures before the defenders had time to reload.

A wild and terrible struggle ensued upon the instant. M'Fadden and his men, with clubbed guns or stout cudgels, fought desperately. Body tumbled over body; blows, shrieks, and curses broke upon the stillness of the night. All was mad havoc and confusion in that thick darkness. The brave defenders of the household fought long and well, but the end came at last. M'Fadden's men were bound and gagged; he himself, feeling that his presence could do no good to them, and driven to a state of frenzy concerning his absent daughter, leaped from one of the windows to escape in search of assistance.

The "Merry Hearts" were masters of the situation.

Oakville was at the mercy of the robber band.

CHAPTER XIII

In which Further Adventures are Related

When Mr. M'Fadden leaped from the window in the manner described, at the close of our last chapter, he had but faint hopes of effecting his escape. He would not have left the house had there been the smallest chance or hope that by remaining he could have given the slightest assistance or have been of the slightest service to his faithful but unfortunate men.

His aim now was to procure help from outside—from his friendly neighbours.

The moment, however, that his feet touched the ground, and that he cast around him one hurried glance, he knew that he had been observed—he felt that he would be pursued.

Fear and despair lent agility and strength to his somewhat stiffening limbs.

A lane which passed through the wood led in the direction of the cottier house, whither he had sent his daughter and his goods.

Towards this lane he instinctively turned, bounding with the nimbleness of youth, and nerved to flight by the noise of pursuing feet behind him,

In the dim light of the October morning his white hair gleamed like snowflakes—a sure guide to the keen eyes of the two ruffians who chased him, thirsting like tigers of the forest for his blood.

The race was a short one.

M'Fadden had reached the outskirt of the wood and felt certain of safety within its impenetrable gloom and deep recesses. But Fate had otherwise decreed. Just as the shadow of the wood was reached, the foremost of the two pursuing robbers closed upon him. As he did so, the ruffian raised his cudgel and brought it down upon M'Fadden's head with crushing force.

There was a dull thud, a sickening groan, and the magistrate fell prostrate upon the earth.

As he fell, the body of the man by whom he had been struck fell stunned and senseless by his side, while the second pursuer, unable to stop in his flight, leaped over the fallen men and into the inky darkness of the wooden lane.

He suddenly drew himself up, but, before he could check the impetus acquired, a dark form leaped upon him and felled him to the earth. Then turning upon the first pursuer, who was now struggling to regain his feet, this mysterious avenger dealt the fellow a blow with the cudgel he carried, which made him, now for the second time, measure his full length upon the sod.

And there the three men lay—silent, unconscious, probably dead, under the canopy of the whispering fir-trees; while the one who had so deftly avenged the attack upon the magistrate knelt quickly by the old gentleman's side, and proceeded to examine his wounds.

Having done this, he glided off into the darkness of the wood.

....

Meanwhile the "Merry Hearts" had not been idle.

They ransacked every corner of Oakville House. But there was nothing to reward search or gratify their love of plunder. No money; no treasure; no plunder of any description—only the four trembling men, bound and gagged, lying in the corner, and wondering what their fate would be.

The outlaws, at a signal whistle from the man who appeared to act as their leader, withdrew to the outside of the house for consultation, leaving two of their number in charge of the disabled prisoners.

On reaching the yard, and the muster being called, two men were discovered to be missing, and a search was immediately ordered to be made.

This search, at once commenced, resulted in the discovery of three prostrate bodies upon the outskirts of the wood.

This appeared to whet still more the dire anger of the band. The prisoners were removed to one of the office-houses at the rear of Oakville House. Then, placing the wounded under a convoy of their own men, the two stricken outlaws and the disabled magistrate were carried away in the direction of Kirkcubbin.

The remainder of the party remained at Oakville until sufficient time had been allowed for the wounded men and their convoy to reach their boat. Then they set fire to the house, and started off to rejoin their companions.

The red glare of the flames shot far upwards and outwards against the black and wintry sky.

The farm servants, gagged and bound, lay helpless in the out-house, where they had been placed, watching the destroying element as tongues of flames leaped madly upward.

Were they to be roasted alive!

The heat grew intense and began to scorch them. They struggled with their bonds, but all their struggles were in vain. The cords cut into their flesh but would not break.

Clouds of fiery sparks and red-hot embers fell around and upon them. Nearer and nearer crept the flames. Fiercer and fiercer grew the heat.

And yet no sign of succour!

The men cried for help. They yelled until their throats were parched, and dry, and burning with pain.

And, all the while, nearer and nearer came the cruel death-dealing flames that threatened to encircle them in their scorching embrace.

Great God! What a terrible death to die!

....

A rush of feet!

A shout from many throats!

Saved—at the last moment.

Help had come at last. Attracted by the lurid glares that shot up into the heavens, the people of the district had leaped from their beds, and, half-clad, had rushed to the scene of the burning. As they neared the spot their speed was increased by the heartrending cries for help uttered by the farm servants. They shouted in return, and bursting into the yard were just in time to drag the poor fellows to a place of safety and out of the jaws of a hideous and horrible death.

And thus the curtain falls upon another act in one of the wild dramas performed towards the close of the last century by members of the band known by the curious misnomer of—

THE MERRY HEARTS OF DOWN.

CHAPTER XIV

A Night of Terror

WHILE the events recorded in the previous chapter were taking place, Miss M'Fadden and the housekeeper were concealed in the vacant cottier house. Personally they felt that they were free from molestation, but nevertheless their anxiety was unspeakable, and their hearts were filled with fear.

In agony of mind they paced the earthen floor of the cottage, scarcely speaking to each other, and straining their ears to catch any sound which might come from the direction of their home. They had sent away the two men servants to see what they could learn.

Momently they expected to receive a message from these men that danger was passed, and that all was well.

But no message came to them. The men did not return.

Once, and once only, the night wind bore to their ear the reverberation of the guns—a sound which to them was full of terror. Nothing further broke the stillness of the night.

Not daring to strike a light, the women were in thick darkness. Time after time they cautiously opened the door of the cottage, straining their eyes and ears, until hope deferred made their hearts sick, and the agony of anxious expectation made them cling to each other for support.

Again they opened the door and peered through the darkness and the trees surrounding the house. The cracking of a branch, as though trodden upon, startled the listening watchers.

"Hush!" whispered Martha; "I see something there beside that fallen tree."

Her keen eyes had discovered the dark outline of a moving figure.

The elder woman strained her eyes in the direction indicated.

"I cannot see anything, dear," she said. "Let us go inside and shut the door."

"Wait a moment," replied Martha, hoping in her heart that friends were near. "Look! There it is again! Ah, now I see a man skulking behind that tree!"

Just then a figure emerged suddenly from the thicket and bounded towards the cottage.

The startled women shrieked, and rushed indoors, their fear rendering them unable to close the door. They huddled into a dark corner, and watched the figure now standing in the doorway.

"Excuse me, leddies, if you please!"

The voice was familiar. Its tone was friendly.

"Who are you?" asked Martha, in a voice quavering from fear.

"Div ye no ken Eddie?" queried the voice. "It was me that cummed tae warn the maister o' what was gaun tae happen—ay, an' it haes happened, ochanee, anee!"

It was Daft Eddie, sure enough.

He had not returned home. Partly from fear of meeting the "Merry Hearts," and partly from the consciousness that he could be of use to the family if near to them, he had concealed himself at the outskirts of the wood at Oakville. There he saw and heard all, and it was his hand which struck down the robbers who had pursued Mr. M'Fadden.

The women were afraid to make answer. They might be in the power of an enemy for aught they knew.

"Dinnae be feered, leddies," said Eddie, after a long pause. "Thae robbin' deevils hae spoiled the nest o' the bonnie doo, an' A hae cum tae warn ye yince mair."

"I do believe that you are our friend," said Martha. "Where is my father? Is he safe? Do tell me!"

"Your faither is at the house," replied Eddie; "an' A hae cum tae road ye till a place o' safety."

"But why did my father not come?" cried Martha, a sudden fear seizing her.

"A dinnae ken," murmured Eddie, in that drawling tone which he always assumed when wishing to evade a direct inquiry.

"Oh, something has happened to him. He may be dead—murdered!" moaned the girl, wringing her hands in agony.

Eddie had feared to excite their alarm, but his very caution and hesitation effected that which he had wished to avoid. He now proceeded to assure the women that Mr. M'Fadden was not dead, but that he had been taken prisoner by the robbers, who would very likely demand a large sum of money before releasing him.

"Martha, dear, what is to be done?" moaned the housekeeper.

"I must go to my father," cried the brave girl.

She tightened her shawl around her as she spoke, and stepped towards the door.

But Eddie stopped her, barring her progress.

"Let me go," she cried, despairingly. "Oh, do take me to my father!"

"That cannae be," said Eddie; "that cannae be, mem."

"And why?"

"There's enuch herm din areaddy," answered Eddie. "A wudnae say but a wheen o' them boys micht cum here aboots lukin' for *you*, an' then the reward wud hae to be doobled, mebbe."

"I will go to my father!" said the girl, resolutely. And she pushed past Eddie.

Mrs. Myrtlebrace stopped her.

"Why would you expose yourself to these men Miss Martha?" she said. "Let us get the horses—they are all ready saddled—and rouse the country."

To this sensible proposal Martha made no objection, but asked Eddie to bring out two of the horses that stood saddled in the adjoining stable.

The lad promptly obeyed. Soon the horses were at the door, and the women in the saddles.

There was now sufficient light to enable the group to recognise each other, and to distinguish objects at some distance.

"To Gilmer's first," said Martha, and the horses moved off.

Eddie evidently meant to follow.

"You must not come with us," said Martha, sharply. "Go back to the house and keep watch there. We shall soon be back with help."

Eddie obeyed, but he did so with evident reluctance.

The women proceeded with the caution rendered necessary by the condition of the road upon which they were. It was an old cart-road, leading to the highway—from which it was nearly a quarter of a mile distant. Gilmer's, the house mentioned by Martha, stood upon the main road, not far from the spot from which they would emerge from the lane they were now traversing.

"I am glad that boy is gone," said Martha; "somehow I suspect he is one of the gang. I don't feel that I can trust him."

"You are a clever girl," replied the housekeeper. "I am just of the same opinion. Now, then, let us make haste."

They had reached the highway and turned to the left.

A word to their horses, and off they galloped.

Both were excellent horsewomen. The exercise was one in which both had for years indulged. They were at home in the saddle.

And now, as they dashed along, with the cool morning air kissing their cheeks, fear began to vanish and hope to rise in their bosoms.

That hope was short-lived!

Ere they had gone three hundred yards, they saw approaching them, from the opposite direction, a man in a gig driving at a breakneck pace, and followed by someone on horseback.

The narrowness of the road obliged the women to slacken speed, and draw off towards one side to allow the travellers to pass.

As they slackened speed, so did the strangers.

Just as they met, the driver of the gig pulled up, at the same time drawing his vehicle right across the road; then, leaping down upon the road, he caught Martha's horse by the bridle. As he did so, he turned to his companion on horseback, and exclaimed, in a voice of triumph:

"In luck this time—here she is!"

Martha was too astounded to give utterance to word or cry.

Not so with Mrs. Myrtlebrace. That worthy lady screamed lustily.

The man who was on horseback dismounted, and flinging his rein over a rail of the gate, came to Martha's side, and, seizing her, dragged her from the saddle.

With an adroitness that told of experience in such things, Martha was gagged with a large handkerchief, her hands secured, and the poor girl hoisted into the gig. The man who previously occupied it jumped up beside her, took his seat, and grasped the reins.

"What'll we dae wi' the auld yin?" asked the horseman.

By the "auld yin" he meant Mrs. Myrtlebrace, who sat with open mouth uttering piercing shrieks.

"Send her to h—l!" shouted the other, giving his horse a sharp cut with the whip as it tore off at a mad pace.

The other fellow mounted his horse, and followed; but as he did so he turned the head of the housekeeper's horse in an opposite direction, and bestowed upon it a merciless cut with his riding whip, sending the pained brute off at a furious gallop.

Then he himself made off in pursuit of the gig.

Poor Martha! She now perceived what a fatal mistake she had made when she doubted Eddie's loyalty. Her face was bowed upon her breast, which heaved with convulsive sobs.

Suddenly she looked up. As she did so, the ruddy glare of the sky over Oakville startled her. She turned upon her companion such an agonising look that his brutal nature was touched, and he removed the handkerchief from the girl's mouth.

"My God!" she cried; "is the house on fire!"

Her companion smiled grimly.

"A daur say it is," he answered, doggedly.

The glare became brighter and brighter, as the flames leaped higher and higher. Martha besought the driver whither he was bound; she begged of him to stop and allow her to dismount. But the fellow never spoke. He whipped his horse to its utmost speed. How far the girl had been carried she knew not. The journey seemed interminable.

Hours seemed to have passed, and still that wild pace was kept up.

At last the driver stopped and jumped from the gig. The horse was reeking and covered with flakes of foam.

Martha looked around, but the place was strange to her. She had been brought to a small evil-looking house that stood in one of the wildest and bleakest parts of the Conlig Hills.

She was lifted from the gig and carried into the hut.

"For God's sake have mercy upon me! Where are you taking me to!" she screamed.

"Ye'll ken that efter a bit," was the gruff answer.

"Take me to my friends, and you will be well rewarded," she pleaded.

"That's the very thing we'll dae, but we'll gang aboot it in oor ain wae," was all the answer or comfort she received.

The fellow untied her hands, and pointing to a door in the wall of the hut, said:

"Ye'll get a bed there, awa an' lie doon. Ye'll be the better o' a rest, A'm thinkin'."

CHAPTER XV

Eddie to the Rescue

GLAD to escape from the presence of her disagreeable companion, Miss M'Fadden gladly went into the apartment which adjoined the kitchen of the old house at Conlig Hills.

Her first care was to fasten the door, which she was enabled to do with a stout wooden bar arranged for that purpose.

Then, for the time being, she breathed more freely and made a hurried survey of her quarters. They were better than one might have expected who looked at the outer apartment. Something told her that the place had been specially prepared for her reception; that her abduction had been planned beforehand, and she shuddered to think of what might yet happen. There were visible traces of a female mind in the disposition of the various little arrangements of the room, which was furnished with a certain amount of taste and comfort. Everything in the place, bed included, was scrupulously clean.

All this Martha took in at a glance, and then, yielding to a sudden revulsion, she burst into tears, and, falling upon her knees, burying her face in her hands, sobbed convulsively. In deep agony of spirit she supplicated aid from on High. Her prayers seemed answered in a measure, for a feeling of hope took possession of her, and, with a calmness that surprised herself, she stretched her tired body upon the bed, and fell asleep.

....

The wintry sun had peeped in at the quaint old window ere Martha opened her eyes.

Sleep had obliterated the recollections of the previous night, and for a moment, following the order of her dreams, she believed herself to be in her own little bedroom at Oakville.

It was indeed but for a single moment. The whitewashed walls, the blue coverlet, the bare, cold, earthen floor, meeting her gaze in quick succession, sent to her heart a sharp and sudden chill.

And then, swift as a flash, all came back to her—the flight from Oakville, the weary watching in the vacant cottage, Daft Eddie, the encounter upon the road, her capture, the cold bleak drive, and her arrival at where she was now a prisoner.

Yes; she felt that she was a prisoner, and, as her thoughts again and again reverted to Eddie she moaned:

"Oh, why did I suspect him? Why did I not trust to that poor boy? What am I to do? What am I to do?"

Battling with her fears like a brave girl as she was, she sprang from her bed exclaiming:

"I will know the worst; I will face my jailers!"

She bathed her face in a basin of cold clean water that stood upon a little table in the bedroom, and felt wonderfully refreshed. Then she undid the bar, opened the door of her closet, and stepped into the outer apartment, or kitchen.

A man whom she had never seen before sat at the fire.

He turned to face the girl as she opened the door.

He was a tall, burly, savage-looking fellow—his countenance ill-favoured and lowering.

It was Commodore Bob!

"That's a fine mornin', miss," he said, looking at her with an impudent leer.

She did not answer him, but stepped quickly towards the outer door.

The Commodore started up and intercepted her.

"Ye cannae gaun oot jist noo," he said, speaking as gently as his rough nature would permit.

"And who will detain me?" demanded the girl, drawing herself up boldly, and looking the ruffian in the eyes unflinchingly.

"Yer humble servant," he said, with an attempt at a bow.

"By what right?" she demanded.

"Ye had better ax nae questions," he answered. "Ye're here noo; an' here ye're likely tae be for a wheen days, at ony rate; so mak yersel' as comfortable as ye can."

Again she attempted to pass him, but he caught her by the wrists, and pushed her back.

"Don't dare to touch me, sir!" she exclaimed, excitedly. "Let me pass! I will not stay here!"

"A think ye wull, mebbe," replied the Commodore, grinning.

His burly form still barred her progress; and, seeing the utter hopelessness of attempting to escape at the present juncture, Martha turned to re-enter the room in which she had passed the night.

As she did so, the Commodore caught her by the shoulder, and wheeling her round suddenly, attempted to kiss her.

The girl uttered a piercing scream, and, maddened by the ruffian's rudeness, involuntarily raised her clenched hand and brought it down with all her force upon his face.

The Commodore staggered—not from the force of the blow, but from its suddenness.

He held the girl back at arm's length, and looked at her admiringly.

"By the hokey!" he exclaimed, "yer a game yin; but A'll hae my kiss for a' that!"

He had hold of her now by both wrists, and her struggles to escape were futile.

He laughed and jeered at her efforts to be released, keeping up a running fire of what he doubtless considered jokes, all the time.

"A kiss for a blow, ye ken, that's what the meinisters preach, isn't it? So ye gied me a blow an' A'll gie ye a kiss. A maun follow the teachin' o' the preachin' for yince in my life at ony rate."

He suddenly grasped her in his arms as he said this. The girl screamed and struggled with all her might. Backwards and backwards he forced her toward the closet. Despite her temporary strength, she was but a child in his grasp, and he seemingly protracted the struggle from a desire to increase her terror. They had reached the doorway, and Martha caught one side of it, holding on as though for dear life. Then the fellow applied his brute strength, and, lifting her bodily in his arms, flung her upon the bed.

"Ah, ha! me leddy!" he cried. "I hev ye now!"

He closed the door with his foot, and, striding to the bedside, glared at the terrified girl like a wild beast.

"Leave me! Go away!" she cried.

The Commodore laughed.

"Niver, my leddy! Niver till A get thae kisses. It maun be twa, noo, or as mony mair as A like."

He meant all he said, and once more seized hold of Martha, whose strength was rapidly sinking.

At that instant there was a loud tramping of horse-hoofs at the outer door.

"D—n!" said the Commodore, "what's in the wun' noo?"

He sprang to the door of the closet and looked out.

What he saw evidently startled him, for he instantly slid the wooden bar into its socket, and, seizing the sashes of the closet window, tore it from the framework. Then, quickly crawling out through the opening thus made, he disappeared.

There was a loud knocking at the outer door, but Martha was now powerless to move or even to utter a cry for help. She had swooned away.

Another minute and the door was broken in. Help had not come too soon. Daft Eddie followed by three brawny farmers rushed into the room.

They uttered a cry of alarm on seeing the prostrate girl, thinking she was dead. Raising her up into a sitting posture, they bathed her face and hands in water. This, together with the current of cold air rushing through the apartment, speedily revived her. Her opening eyes fell upon friendly, well-known faces, and she gave utterance to a cry of joy and thankfulness.

It was some time before she could talk calmly and coherently, for her young nerves had been terribly unstrung. As she grew stronger, mutual explanations were made. Eddie told how he had encountered the housekeeper and learned from her that her young mistress had been forcibly carried off. She had given him her horse to follow in pursuit and do what he could to render her assistance.

Eddie told his story in short disjointed sentences, for he was terribly excited, and his recital of it occupied a considerable time.

We shall relate it in a more connected and intelligible style.

Mounting the horse placed at his disposal by the housekeeper, Eddie followed the gig at a safe distance to its destination. Concealing himself and his steed he watched the house for fully an hour, when, having heard no sounds coming from it, he concluded that the young lady was to be kept there all night. He then galloped off towards Bangor, where resided one or two farmers known to him, and after some delay succeeded in obtaining assistance, with the result which we have seen.

CHAPTER XVI

The Mill Glen

A LITTLE to the north-west of the romantic and ancient town of Newtownards there bubbles and bursts, and ripples, a tiny little rivulet, running headlong towards Strangford Lough. This little river is so small and insignificant that it hardly deserves the name. Yet that same little river has seen many wonderful sights, and in the days gone by, the glen through which it wimples has been the scene of many strange events. It is of this glen of which we would now speak, but a slight description of the place will he necessary for the proper understanding of the events about to be recorded.

This little burn, or rivulet, rising in the rough, heather-clad hills that gird in the smiling valleys of the Ards, runs down, gathering strength as it goes till it is joined by another small stream, at the head of the glen at Tullygardy. These two streams, thus wedded in their waters, course downwards over a pebbly bottom, through a deep and tangled glen, towards the town. After proceeding onwards for a little way, it makes a wheel to the right, as if to make believe that any person who would imagine that it was going towards the sea was very much mistaken. However, by-and-by, the brook, appearing by degrees to change its mind, circles round the town, and at last empties itself into the sea about half a mile down the shore road, at a place now called the "Flood-gates."

The two streams at their junction in the glen form a figure not unlike the letter Y. At this junction is a lofty rock rising up almost out of the bed of the rivers. On every side in the immediate neighbourhood the scenery is picturesque and wild in the extreme. Ridge upon ridge of great heathery mountains rise around; the summit of each successive ridge is crowned with a cairn of rocks and stones, placed there too long ago to be remembered. At a short distance from this spot, over the mountains, are the Conlig Mines, from which lead and silver ore were then plentifully extracted. These lead mines supplied work for many workers, and already the secret organisation which we have described had made its appearance among the miners of Conlig.

In this bleak, rugged, and bosky tarn, hazels and stunted oaks grew up in wild luxuriance and confusion. The little stream bubbled and thundered through numerous gullies, fissures, and falls, making the solitude as drearily poetical and romantic as might well be. At the present day, the place may still be seen, but that ruthless scavenger Old Time has made many changes. Science and economy have destroyed the wildness of the scenery, by creating dams, the overfall of which now turns the busy mills. The tangled gorse and furze, and whins, and hazel are in a great part uprooted; a sheet of water flows over the spot where once the rabbit frisked; but the place still bears many traces of its former wild and picturesque grandeur. The lead mines are abandoned on the hill—their shafts still open, their workshops and houses torn down, the shale and earth lying round about in mounds—a feeling of desolation overhangs it all, and strikes the summer tourist with a heartfelt awe as he wanders round the dreary, barren scene.

At the junction of the rivers, as we have said, there stood, and stands, a lofty rugged rock. It was midnight, and at the base of this rock stood two dark figures. Their presence at that hour in this wild place could be for no good purpose. Even in broad daylight they might have stood there among the hazels securely hidden within the bosom of the glen, for very few of the inhabitants of the New Town ever dived into these impenetrable wilds. They were dressed in the rough clothes of miners and were engaged in earnest conversation.

"Dae ye ken wha it is the Killinchy boys are bringin' us the nicht?" said one of the men in a whisper.

"No, but it maun be some ane wi' a power o' gowd," said his companion.

"How much is on his head, did ye hear?"

"Five hunner."

"Five hunner! That's a power o' money. A dae hope," the speaker continued, "that they hae na taen some ane that the Gover'ment will be lukin' efter."

"Why, man, dae ye fear fur the guid cause no prosperin'?"

"Fear or no fear, Johnny, it'll be a dear day fur us if our wee plans are fun oot."

There was a long pause during which each of the men appeared to be busy with his own thoughts. They moved not—they scarcely seemed to breathe, so silent and rigid did they stand.

A low whistle was heard creeping over the Glen.

The two men sank slowly on the ground among the underwood waiting and watching in silence.

At length footsteps were heard approaching the place, and, the men raising their heads among the willows, listened to the sounds. The steps approached nearer and nearer. Then one of the men, putting his hands to his mouth, uttered a close imitation of the whirr of the snipe, startled by the footsteps of the travellers. The signal was answered by the cry of the owl.

"To-whit-to-hoo!"

"It's a' richt," said the men together; and, rising up, they were joined by three men.

The trio that approached was a peculiar one. Two men of stalwart frame led or guided, by the arms, an old blindfolded man over the rough and tangled path.

The men having exchanged some private conversation, the two whom we have first seen turned and conducted the new comers up the Glen. When they had gone about fifty yards they knelt down, and, drawing back a quantity of boughs, brambles and brushwood, that were growing from the bank of the stream, exposed the entrance of a small cave. Into this cave the blindfolded man was conducted. Inside this cavern they felt themselves secure; but the miners, by some means known to themselves, caused the solid rock to open, and the five wanderers in that dreary place passed inwards into the very bowels of the earth.

The door of massive rock swung slowly back behind them, shutting them out entirely from the outer world. A light was soon kindled, revealing the interior of the cave. In one corner was a couch, or bed of straw and horse rugs. A stool and table were all the rest of the furniture it contained. The roof was high and rocky and down the green sides of this gloomy cavern trickled a constant stream of water. The close, damp smell was overpowering, and the cold of that damp hole sent a chill through the frame of the old man.

The two miners having disguised their faces with mud from the floor and walls, each of the four men drew from his pocket a pistol, and, examining the priming, stood round the blinded man, their pistols pointed towards the man's breast. If they had brought him to this place to kill him no better scene of execution could be found, for here no sound or flash of powder could be heard or seen, and the corpse might rot to carrion in this damp charnel house.

Such was not their object, however. By a dexterous stroke of a knife, the cord which bound their victim's hand was cut, and the old man stood still and shivering as the circulation began to return to his hands and arms.

"Ye can tak aff the blin'faul noo, Mr. M'Fadden," said one of the men.

M'Fadden, for it was he, tore off the bandage from his eyes.

Four men, their pistols pointing towards his breast, stood facing him.

"Has my hour, then, come at last?" said he, with a bitter sigh, covering his face with his hands.

"Na, na, sur; Guid be thankit, ye're weel an' daein' weel."

"Then why this menacing and torture?"

"Fur yer ain guid an' oors, sur," said the speaker of the party.

"How so—where am I?"

"That's jist ane o' the things we daurnae tell ye, sur," was the reply.

"Oh, my daughter, my daughter! Speak, men, for the love of God. Where is my daughter? Say, what do you want? My life is little use to you; my money—take it, and let me go, but spare my poor Martha!"

The old man's grief overcame him, and he wept like a child. At length, recovering himself with an effort, he turned towards his persecutors again.

"Why do you stand there with your pistols pointed at me? Ha! cowards! You want my money. Take all I have and let me go. This cursed place would stifle a man! Oh! for a few stout boys from Ballyeasborough!" And the old man, fairly broken, sank down upon the couch of straw and groaned aloud.

"Oor body has fixed your ransom at five hunner, sur, an' it's no in oor power tae tak less. If ye want writin' paper fur yer friens, sur, tak this, an' your stay here may be a short ane."

"The shorter the better," said M'Fadden. "Show me the paper."

The paper was reached to him, with pen and ink, which the robber had brought with him for the purpose. For a few minutes the old man's numbed and trembling hand was heard scratching on the paper. When he had written the note he folded it, and hastily addressed it to Mr. Matthews, Ballywalter.

The robber took the letter, and, opening it, read it aloud: "My dear friend, pay the bearer £500 for me. I am in the hands of a gang of thieves, who have demanded this sum for my ransom. They took me by water to an old ruined house some place about Killinchy, beneath which a regular labyrinth of caverns exist. Having found out the locality, they brought me away again blindfolded, and I am now concealed in a cavern, God knows where. Clap on all your spies and scouts, and follow the bearer of the money; but pay it, I implore you, at once. Look after Martha till I am restored, if ever I may be, to my life and liberty. My poor girl! God bless you—T. M'Fadden."

"A kind note, Mr. M'Faddyen; but ye show a quare soort o' generosity for yer life an' liberty," said the robber, and tore the letter into shreds, and dictated the following to the trembling magistrate: "I have fallen into trouble in a house in Belfast. Send me by the bearer £500 at once. My life depends upon it. Act with all despatch and secrecy. God bless you—"

"Noo, put in as much as ye like about yer dochter," said he, and the old man wrote.

"Good," said the outlaw, reading the letter. "Now, you will remain here till we have got the means o' your release."

"But what pledge have I that you will release me when you get the money?"

"The word o' yin o' th' 'Merry Hearts o' Down'; an' if that winnae dae, ye can get nae ither. There's a bed in yon corner. Tak my advice, sur, and tak a sleep. Oor frien's here'll gie ye plenty o' baith meat and drink."

The miners produced a quantity of coarse bread, some cold roasted wildfowl, a large bottle of poteen, or illicit whiskey, and a pitcher of water.

"We were taul' tae feed ye weel, sur, and we hae gi'en ye the best the hills o' the Ards afford. Gin the morn ye wull have plenty o' licht through the hole in the roof o' this cave, an' we wull be wi' ye aboot dayli'go wi' mair. Noo ye maun eat, drink, and be merry on the guid things afore ye."

Having delivered themselves of these cheering expressions, the secret spring was touched from the inside. The door in the rock opened and the four men stepped out into the outer cave, leaving the almost heartbroken man in solitude, darkness and despair.

CHAPTER XVII

A Reign of Terror

THE people of Ballyeasborough and of the surrounding districts were naturally in a condition of the wildest alarm. The tidings of the sudden disappearance of Mr. M'Fadden and of the burning of his house spread like wildfire, and excitement of the most intense kind prevailed.

That excitement, amounting almost to a panic, was intensified by the doings of the "Merry Hearts," for the band, like wild beasts who had tasted blood, seemed to pursue the depredations with a fury and boldness uncontrollable.

Day by day reports of fresh outrages reached the ears of the people. Those who lived in solitary, out-of-the-way places lay down in their beds at night in terror lest they should be attacked before morning dawned, and but few went abroad after nightfall unarmed.

At one time it was reported that the mail-coach from Downpatrick to Belfast had been robbed. Now a house was plundered at Saintfield, the inhabitants being left gagged and bound till daylight. Now a man was murdered in Loughries Moss and buried, no one knew where, till his body was afterwards discovered. Again, a schooner lying off Portaferry was boarded, the hands on board gagged and bound in the usual fashion, and the cargo pillaged—for the "Merry Hearts" carried on their lawless doings both by land and sea.

The freebooters were not in every instance successful. On many occasions they were foiled by cunning; upon others they were beaten off and compelled to seek safety in flight. One night they broke into the dwelling house of an old man named Morrison, near to Newtownards, and compelled him to open all the drawers of an old-fashioned secretaire that stood in the corner of the kitchen beside the fireplace. While the old man was engaged in doing this, he managed adroitly to gather up a handful of guineas which were in one of the drawers, and to drop them into a meal-barrow that was close at hand. The golden coins sank in the meal and the robbers were outwitted.

Scores of stories could be told of the depredations of the "Merry Hearts", most of which have been handed down from father to son, and are often talked about at the present day.

But to resume our story.

The sudden disappearance of good Mr. M'Fadden and the abduction of his daughter were events to cause more than a nine days' wonder.

Where were they?

What had befallen them?

Were they murdered?

It was some little time before the people of Ballyeasborough could look calmly at the position of affairs. When at length they were able to do so, it was decided that immediate steps and prompt measures should be taken to unravel the mystery.

....

Some days after the disappearance of Mr. M'Fadden, Mr. Matthews, of Ballywalter, had a visitor.

He was a young man, apparently of the farming class; rather good-looking, but shy and irresolute in manner.

The visitor was no other than our old acquaintance, William Douglas, who had been selected as the person to convey the letter written by Mr. M'Fadden in the Glen Cave.

The instructions given to Douglas were brief, but easily understood. They were to the following effect: "Deliver the letter to Matthews only; get the money, and bring it here. If you fail, or attempt treachery, your life will be the forfeit."

And Willie started upon his errand with a sad heart, and possessed with gloomy forebodings.

The drawing of the skull upon the hearthstone was ever before his eyes!

Little wonder that his heart beat audibly, and that he looked shy and irresolute as he knocked at Mr. Matthew's door and was admitted to that gentleman's presence.

"Come in, my man," said Mr. Matthews, encouragingly, as Douglas stood peering in at the parlour door.

Willie nervously entered the apartment, drew the letter from his pocket, and handed it to Mr. Matthews without speaking.

By a motion of his hand Mr. Matthews invited Willie to be seated. Then he tore the letter open and read it attentively.

Having finished the perusal of the missive, he fixed a scrutinising gaze upon Douglas, and said:

"Before giving you an answer to this letter I have a few words to say to you."

Willie made no answer, but glanced furtively round the room.

"I do not ask you," went on Mr. Matthews, "if you are one of this mean and cowardly band of fellows who attack the houses of innocent, sleeping inhabitants of this county. The very fact of your coming here as their messenger tells me at once that you are connected with them; that you know their nefarious plans, and that you expect to reap a rich harvest by murder and robbery—"

Willie started involuntarily. The schemes of his co-conspirators had not until now been presented to him in that light. He felt alarmed, not of any personal injury, but his kindly, noble nature rebelled against the party he had sworn to support, and he felt appalled at the position which he now occupied.

Mr. Matthews instantly perceived the impression which his words had made and continued:

"I will not offer you gold as a temptation or inducement to betray your confederates or to violate the oath which you have doubtless taken; but, if there is any tie in Heaven or on earth that you hold sacred, I adjure you to leave these bandits, and make what reparation you can in the future for the misdeeds which you may have committed in the past."

"Sur," said Willie, in a voice that trembled with emotion, "A can dae naething! A'm ordered tae cum here fur money, an' they wad kill me if A tried tae prove fause tae the cause."

"The Cause!" exclaimed Mr. Matthews, indignantly. Then, suddenly recovering himself, he went on:

"Though it were to save the life of my dearest friend, I would not ask you to be foresworn; but I warn you to take care. I have obtained certain clues now which I shall not fail to follow up; and, should I succeed in discovering this gang of robbers, your own safety will depend upon the assistance you may give. Think over what I have said, my man, for I don't believe you are as bad as the rest. I will now give you this money."

The speaker left the room, and returned after an absence of a few minutes, carrying in his hand a small canvas bag.

"Here," he said, "count your cash."

As he spoke he emptied upon a table the contents of the little bag—a heap of bright, golden guineas.

Not another word passed between them. Douglas, with shaking hand, counted the money, but so confused was he that he really could not have said what was the amount. He put it back into the bag; thrust it into his breast; buttoned up his jacket, and stepped out of the door which Mr. Matthews stood holding open.

CHAPTER XVIII

A Highway Adventure

WITH rapid strides, and looking neither to the right nor to the left, Willie Douglas pushed on towards Kirkcubbin.

Had he looked behind he would have seen that six men followed at a distance.

Were they friends or foes?

Every now and then he put his hand upon his breast as though to secure the gold in its position there.

At a turn of the road he was accosted by a miserable-looking beggar, of huge proportions and gruesome aspect.

It was a wild, secluded part of the road—a dangerous place for one to meet a troublesome wayfarer.

The hedges on either side of the road were high, and threw a dark shadow over the roadway.

No house was in sight.

The beggarman accosted Douglas, when they met, after the custom of the country, "bidding him the time of day."

Douglas made no answer, so absorbed was he with his own thoughts.

The next moment, however, he was suddenly brought to a stand by the beggarman stepping right in front of him, and placing his hand upon his shoulder.

"Weel, what luck?" he asked.

There was no possibility of mistaking the voice!

The beggarman was Commodore Bob!

Douglas was not in a pleasant mood, but he could not refrain from laughing at the appearance of the Commodore in his queer disguise.

"It's a' richt," Willie answered. "A hae gotten the money, but A'm hert sorry A ever had ocht tae dae wi' the jab."

"Hoo's that? Haes the auld cove frichtened ye?"

"It's no that he haes frichtened me a'thegither, but he haes din mair. He has talkit till me aboot this dirty wark till am fairly sick o' it, and gin A had this jab din, A'll quat the cursed 'Merry Hearts'."

"Ha, ha!" laughed the beggarman.

There was a wild, weird sound in that laugh which well-nigh curdled the blood in Willie's veins.

"Yer ower thin-skinned, Douglas," said the Commodore. "Here, tak a drap o' this tae rise yer speerits."

So saying he produced a black bottle from his wallet and handed it to Willie, who required no pressing to take a hearty pull of Alick Martin's liquor.

"A'll be the better o' that," he said, handing back the bottle.

"Ye wull, shairly. Noo, show me the money."

Douglas produced the bag of gold.

At the chink of the coin the Commodore's eyes fairly blazed as with a fierce desire.

"Pit it back," he said. "Pit it by safe; watch the pocket ye keep it in for fear ye loss it."

Douglas replaced the bag in his breast.

As he did so, his head was bent forward, and his eyes averted from his companion.

Then once more that fierce light flashed in the eyes of the Commodore, and a murderous expression settled upon his evil face. Quick as a flash he raised a stout cudgel which he carried in his right hand and brought it down with terrific force upon Willie's head.

The sound of that blow was sickening—like the crash of a man's boot through a piece of rotten timber.

Douglas staggered wildly across the road, with a cry of pain and terror.

The hot blood spurted from a deep gash in his head, filling his eyes and bathing his face and neck. He felt the blindness of death creeping over his eyes, and the numbness of dissolution seizing upon his limbs.

Still wildly staggering, he flung his arms about him, vaguely and in frenzy.

The bloody spray had dashed into the Commodore's face, blinding him for an instant, and forcing him to wipe his eyes with the back of his hand. Then, lifting his weapon again, he dealt a second murderous blow upon his victim.

Willie fell upon the road, literally bathed in blood.

And there he lay—silent, motionless.

All this had occupied but a few seconds; and then the Commodore, smiling grimly at his work, threw down his bludgeon, and dropping upon his knees thrust his hand into the breast pocket of the prostrate and bleeding man.

CHAPTER XIX

Lynch Law

THE murderous attack made by the Commodore upon Willie Douglas, as related in the previous chapter, was witnessed by the six men to whom reference has already been made.

On leaving Ballyeasborough these watchers, for such they were, had taken to the fields, and, keeping, at a safe distance, had followed Douglas, the intervening hedge securely screening them from view.

Their object was to track Douglas to his destination, and if possible to discover the gang upon whose mission he had been sent.

They were totally unprepared for the wayside tragedy enacted before their very eyes and before they could leap over the hedge to interfere.

But now, with a loud whoop, they scrambled through the hedge and surrounded the murderous highwayman.

The Commodore leaped to his feet with a sudden cry of alarm.

In his left hand he held the bag of gold, wrenched from his victim's pocket; in his right hand he held his blood-stained cudgel!

A single instant was sufficient for him to take in the situation and surroundings.

"Damn ye!" he shouted; and swiftly swinging his bludgeon round his head he felled to the earth the man who stood nearest him.

The others held back for an instant as though dazed by the suddenness of the attack.

The instant's respite was sufficient for the Commodore. Flourishing his bludgeon round his head, and leaping over the prostrate body of the man whom he had felled, he dashed down the road uttering shouts of defiance.

Three of the men started in pursuit, while two remained to look after the injured.

Commodore Bob did not long keep to the highway. A few paces brought him to a place where the thorn hedge was less dense. Against this spot he flung himself with sufficient force to make a passage for his huge body, and then he darted off across the fields in which he found himself.

The three men followed at full speed, but the Commodore was rapidly increasing the distance between them. He possessed vast strength and tore along with big strides and enormous speed. But the beggarman's outfit began soon to encumber him, and tearing off the big cloak which formed part of his disguise, he flung it into a ditch.

On he went with renewed vigour, and on pressed his pursuers, panting for breath, and fairly frenzied with rage.

The shades of evening were beginning to fall over hill and dale.

If ever the Commodore prayed, he prayed for darkness, the thick darkness of night. He was beginning to grow faint, and darkness seemed his only chance of escape. He knew well that if he were overtaken certain death would be his fate.

He ran, apparently, not knowing or heeding where he went. One thing was evident, however. Every now and then a figure would come in view, and, taking in the situation, join in the chase.

The Commodore saw this and inwardly cursed himself for not sooner turning upon his pursuers and attempting to disable them.

As one after another joined in the chase, the three original pursuers gasped forth one word—"Murder!" The word was sufficient to secure the aid of everyone with whom he came in contact.

And now, right ahead, a plantation came in sight. Its appearance afforded the hunted man a gleam of hope. Could he but hold out and reach the shelter of that wood he might escape. But his strength was failing fast.

Between him and the wood was a small cottier house. Towards this he dashed, followed now by fully twenty men who panted for his blood.

A young girl and an old woman, who were apparently the only occupants of the house, came to the door, attracted by the sounds of the pursuit.

As the murderer approached them they shrieked and fled, frightened at the strange apparition.

He dashed into the house and clashed the door behind him, and bolted it.

The crowd surrounded him in an instant, and rushed towards the door; but the savage, driven to bay, turned upon his pursuers, and with a heavy hedge-hook in his hand, which he found in the corner of the house, he waited for their onset.

He opened the door, and stood thus before them.

There was no one who would rush in and meet certain death.

Those behind cried "Forward!" and those before cried "Back!"

There was a pause for some time, during which the sinews in the lithe Herculean robber were quivering with the exertion he had undergone.

A number of the besiegers, scrambling in by a window in the rear of the cottage, leaped on him from behind and bore him to the earth, while the other party was diverting his attention by pretending to make an attack on him in the front.

With great difficulty he was secured, and an obliging neighbour ran for a halter which he volunteered to lend to the prisoner.

Better counsel, however, prevailed, and Bob was led, naked and bleeding, as he was torn with the whins, thorns and briars through which he had passed, back to Ballywalter Park. The money also was recovered from his possession, for which he had committed the foul crime of murdering his brother conspirator in defiance of all oaths of brotherhood.

"Alas!" said Mr. Matthews, as the money was returned to him, "which of the band will now come for this cursed money after what has happened? Poor M'Fadden must remain a prisoner, too, for many a day to come in the hands of these men."

Bob was given over to the hands of Justice. On the morrow he was placed on a cart for the purpose of being conveyed to Downpatrick Jail. He never reached his destination.

The stalwart farmers of the Ards attacked the cart containing the prisoner. The yeomen who were guarding him, not unwillingly retreated, leaving cart and prisoner at the mercy of the mob, and the mob treated the prisoner after its own fashion.

The Commodore, as he was torn out of the cart, read his fate in the flashing eyes and angry faces around him. A night of rest had restored his strength and he determined not to die without a struggle. Snatching a stick from the hand of a man beside him he brings it down upon the head of its owner, and then with a yell he makes a general onslaught. He knows it is all useless; that he is fearfully outnumbered and sure to be overcome. Yet he fights with the fury of a tiger. One man seizes him from behind; another seizes the uplifted arm; a third member of the crowd of vigilantees deals him a blow in the face that almost fells him and brings a stream of blood, while others seize his legs and arms, crying for a rope.

In the hands of a dozen men he is, with scores of others pressing forward to get at him—some anxious to tear him limb from limb without more ado, the others eager to reserve him for the rope and the limb of a tree—the Commodore still struggles, fights, and kicks in his impotent desperation, the only result to bring more punishment upon himself, until he is a sickening sight, bloody, battered and bruised.

"A rope! A rope!" hoarsely shouts the swaying, struggling, maddened crowd.

"Here ye ir!" is the answering shout, as a big burly young farmer presses forward, waving a stout new rope over his head.

With a cheer the crowd opens up a passage for him.

There is an ancient tree hard by the roadside near Kirkcubbin, whose knotty, gnarled limbs have defied the storms of ages. One of these limbs then stretched out over the road, although it has since been removed.

Under this branch the struggling wretch was drawn by his infuriated captors, and held there while the rope was being prepared. Its strands were new and hard, and the noose refused to run freely.

"Creesh it!" cried one of the crowd; and the ready joke made even that angry crowd laugh.

From a farm-house that stood near, a pot of cart grease was instantly brought, and ready hands smeared the rope most liberally.

"Try it noo!" shouted someone in the crowd.

It worked beautifully.

"String him up!"

"Awa' wi' him!"

"Gie him a swing!"

These, and other shouts, filled the air.

The noose was slung over the man's neck, and the other end of the rope was dexterously thrown over the big stout limb of the tree.

A dozen hands grasped the loose end.

All was ready!

"Gie him a chance!" shouted one of the ringleaders in this lynching scene. "Ax him whaur Mister M'Fadyen is!"

In an instant calmer reason succeeds the excited fury that has become contagious.

"Dinna kill me!" pleads the Commodore, the momentary hush giving him courage.

"Whaur's M'Fadyen?"

"A dinnae ken," whined the wretch, looking in vain for a single friendly or pitying look in the sea of faces that surrounds him.

"String him up!" yelled a large, heavy man with a big slouch hat.

The Commodore pleaded for mercy. He became almost incoherent in his appeals, but the temper of the crowd was for a short shrift and a speedy hanging.

"Pull!"

The rope is taut; the man dangles from the tree, and a hoarse murmur sweeps through the crowd. Almost immediately the executioners let him down again. They want to hear his confession before he strangles. He appears to be dead, but he soon revives.

"Will you confess?"

He answers by a shake of the head, and up he goes again, and down almost as soon again. This treatment loosens his tongue, and in a voice that can be heard only by those nearest him he makes some rambling statement.

Although all cannot hear what he says, it takes but a moment for one to repeat it to the other, and an incredulous murmur runs through the crowd.

"What shall we do with him?" calls out a deep voice from beside the trembling wretch. The answer comes from a hundred throats in chorus:

"String him up!"

And the executioners follow the command. Again the body dangles from the branch. A shudder seizes the frame of the pinioned man, the death struggle of strangulation, and Commodore Bob is dead!

CHAPTER XX

The Kirkcubbin Doctor

THE two men who remained with Willie Douglas, who had been left for dead by the wayside, and also to look after the condition of their companion, whose skull had been well-nigh cracked by the Commodore's bludgeon, raised the bodies up and laid them against the side of the ditch.

Then one of them ran to Kirkcubbin for help whilst the other remained to keep guard over the sufferers.

The town was soon reached, and the inhabitants were speedily aroused. Doctor Black, who was then living in Kirkcubbin, went to the spot immediately. He shook his head gravely as he examined the bleeding and battered skull of Douglas.

Next he made a hurried survey of the other man.

"There's been rough work here," he said; "but this fellow will be all right in a minute or two if some of you will throw a little cold water on his face."

Willing hands did as directed; and the man, who had been merely stunned, quickly recovered.

Then the doctor transferred his attention to Willie.

"Beautiful dislocation!" he murmured, as he rapidly passed his fingers over the jaws of the prostrate man.

"Temporal bone smashed," he went on; "brain protruding here—splendid case for trepanning—nose broken—why, it's the loveliest case I've seen since I left the hospitals."

The doctor positively chuckled with satisfaction.

"Not dead, not a bit of it," he continued. "I'll take him home to my own house, treat him there, and send a report of his case to the *Journal*."

By Dr. Black's directions a door was brought; and, stretched out upon it, Willie was taken to the doctor's residence, so that the worthy practitioner might experiment upon him alone and unchallenged. If the man should recover, it would be a triumph of skill. If he died—well, so much information would be gained and "The Faculty" would be the richer by a report in the *Medical Journal* entitled: "Experiments upon a man whose skull was smashed."

Thus thinking, Dr. Black had, as above stated, Willie removed to his house, where a bed was speedily prepared for the sufferer. The doctor's wife was a tender-hearted, sympathetic woman, and her sympathies were quickly aroused on behalf of Douglas. She did not enter into "the beauty" of the case as did her husband. She pitied the poor stricken man, and did what she could for him out of pure love for humanity, while the doctor, getting ready his instruments and note-book, prepared himself for unusual exertion in his art.

Dr. Black was a merry little man, with a merry twinkle in his eyes, and a pleasant, good-humoured expression of countenance. He was vastly popular with all the people in the neighbourhood, being kind and courteous towards the most humble, and displaying no trace of sycophancy towards the better classes. He was, in truth, a genuine Good Samaritan, a man who yet lives in the memory of thousands though his ashes repose in the Glastry graveyard, so ardently did Dr. Black love his profession. Kindhearted as he was he could not help feeling, as he stood by the side of Willie Douglas, that a fortunate circumstance had brought to him this bruised and broken atom of humanity upon which to exert his utmost skill and learning. The feelings which stirred the good doctor's heart were somewhat akin to those that move the soul of the antiquarian when he discovers an antique Irish Urn, or a farthing coined during the reign of the good Queen Anne.

....

Days and weeks passed. Willie Douglas still lay in the house of Dr. Black—but he could not have been in better hands. Long had he hovered upon the threshold of death, but the grim messenger struck not the final blow.

The doctor would scarcely take rest, so anxious was he to do battle with the ghostly spectre that hovered round his patient, eager to bear him off to the land of shades and spirits. "Medical skill must triumph," said the doctor; and he prided himself that he possessed the requisite skill to triumph.

At times the thought occurred to him that even if his man did recover he must be handed over to justice; that in all likelihood the unfortunate fellow would die upon the scaffold as an atonement for his doings with the "Merry Hearts of Down."

But what of that!

The doctor would do his duty.

Hopes of the recovery of Douglas were now strong. His poor wife had found him out. The discovery was to her a frightful shock, and all but deprived her of her reason. Ever since, by day and night, she had nursed her husband with a devotion that could not fail to excite the admiration of Dr. Black and his amiable spouse.

The cottage by the seashore was tenantless; Willie's wife and child were both beside him.

It was long, however, before the suffering man could recognise his dear ones that kept unceasing watch over him. When at length he did recognise his wife, the scene was an affecting one. His dull eyes sparkled for a moment, lighting his deadened features, and his indistinct, incoherent ramblings became sensible and coherent. It was like a sudden gleam of sunshine bursting from behind a dark bank of clouds, and as the wife kissed and caressed her husband her tears of joy fell upon her white face. He made an effort to rise in the bed, but his head fell back upon the pillow, and then, as he eagerly extended his arms, he cried out:—

"Is that you, Maggie? Whaur did ye come frae? A'm gaun tae leave you an' the bairn, Maggie. It'll be caul' dark weather tae lie in Killinchy, honey. The boys'll hae a hard job carryin' me up the knowe-head in the frost, though A'm no sae heavy as A was. The caul' Hame Brae'll no—whaur are ye noo, Maggie? Ye're awa' again."

Consciousness had again departed, and the poor fellow's mind went rambling away back into the dead past, to the days of his early life.

"We'll wan'er nae mair by the Shillan hill, Maggie, nor sit at nichts by the big stanes o' Jerusalem. There's a keen breeze frae the sea, an' the waters o' Cowan are swellin'. Rin, Maggie, for A'm ower weak, and tell the boys no till gaun out till the mac'rel the nicht. There's an angry sough aboot the waters, an' the gulls are skreghin' ower Cadoo."

"There now; I told you so," said the doctor. "You see he is getting better."

Mrs. Douglas saw nothing of the kind; but she curtsied to the doctor and said: "Yes, sir."

"When he came here he was too weak even to talk. We'll bring him round, Mrs. Douglas, never fear; we'll bring him round—we'll bring him round."

And the kindhearted old man rubbed his hands with delight, and pressed a guinea into the hand of the poor famished wife. When he had performed this act of charity the doctor commenced to talk very hard, whilst Mrs. Douglas burst into a flood of tears.

Hush! The patient begins to talk again. This time he was among the "Merry Hearts," and the scene of the outrage was re-enacted.

"Och, och, it's a sair nicht tae turn the puir folk oot o' their hoose. There's nae money aboot the place, an' Bob swears he'll burn it."

He started up in his delirium, and gazed frantically around him.

"Whaur's M'Fadden?" he asked. "Hae they taen him tae the cave aboon Newtown—the cave at the tap o' the glen whaur the hazels grow ower the water, an' the wee burn comes wimplin' till the sea? Guid help us, it's as bad as the auld cave at the ghaist hole at Comer! There's rats there—ay, tarble rats. There they are—hie, Midge, Midge!—rats, Midge!" Then he fell back exhausted in his bed.

The doctor extended his charity not only to his patient, but, hearing the story of their lives from the poor wife, and how their peace and happiness were blighted by the secret band, he started a subscription. He prevailed upon many of the gentlemen in the neighbourhood, and a considerable sum of money was shortly raised among them for her support in the meantime.

From the ravings of the stricken man much information was gained.

The doctor was an apt scholar, and picked out from among the chaff the grains of wheat. By this time he learned where M'Fadden was confined. He became acquainted also with the names of the conspirators, and their secret doings. He also learned that this secret band must have made considerable advances throughout the Ards, and that many lodges were located over different parts of the country.

On communicating to Mr. Matthews the information he had gained from the delirium of Willie Douglas that gentleman with the rash impetuosity for which he was so remarkable in his time, at once determined to beard the lion in his den. As there was no person to say against him, he had it very much his own way. His proposition was carried out on the understanding that action should be taken immediately, but as quietly as possible.

It was resolved not to wait for the intervention of the police. The Royal Irish Constabulary were not scattered over the county at this period as they are now. In fact, if they had had existence, the question remained if the "peelers" had the requirements that were then essential in Mr. Matthew's eyes. He undertook to bring seven "men who would face the devil." We really cannot say how the members of our present force would behave if called upon to discharge this duty among their others. The hardy tenants of Mr.

M'Fadden from Ballyeasborough joined as a matter of course and also a good number of the inhabitants of the country adjacent.

One morning the men were summoned to assemble at Kirkcubbin. There they were asked to join the expedition. Ten minutes afterwards they all marched towards Newtownards.

Daft Eddie, who either knew, or pretended to know more of the way than any of the others, accompanied them, by the permission of Mr. Matthews, between whom and the lad a great attachment had sprung up.

It was a clear, bright morning in early spring. The sun arose with more than his usual pomp and splendour out of his misty ocean bed over the placid waters of Lough Cowan. The larks, high overhead, discoursed their full tide of song in the warm rays of the early sun. The yellow whins that fringed the roadside with the delicious perfume of spring held many a merry warbler, carolling forth its song of joyfulness that summer was coming once more to gladden the earth. On such a morning and amid such scenes the procession moved onward to discover the cave of the robbers, root out the terrible band, and rescue the prisoner from their grasp.

In number or in grandeur the procession was not imposing, but in willing courageous hearts in a warm devotion to the cause, it was an army. First rode Mr. Matthews, of Ballywalter, a sword by his side, and two pistols ominously protruding from the holsters of his saddle. Beside him rode the stout old doctor, in a prodigious good humour. His patient was so far recovered that the doctor was enabled to leave him. Immediately behind them rode Eddie on a little pony.

Behind these again there followed a strange and motley crew, consisting of about thirty men. They were clad in their ordinary working garments and armed with a strange medley of accoutrements. Scythes, reaping-hooks, hedge-hooks, pistols, guns, and old cutlasses (many of which did service with the smugglers round the coast) were the most common weapons; but crowbars, sledge hammers, and large sticks of ash and blackthorn were also to be seen flourishing among the crowd, as its bearer knocked down an imaginary "Merry Heart."

In this order they proceeded through Greyabbey and all along the shore to Newtown. Now and then a cheer broke out from the crowd as they thought of the sufferings of Mr. M'Fadden and his daughter.

The stout farmers of the Ards were burning with desire to rescue M'Fadden and demolish the robbers' cave in Tullynagardy Glen. We shall see how they succeeded.

CHAPTER XXI

To the Rescue

IN our last chapter we left the sturdy band marching to the rescue, or the attempted rescue, of Mr. M'Fadden.

When they reached Newtown it was still the early morning.

As they entered the town they were surrounded by a wondering and enquiring crowd who fancied that a rising must be at hand.

The news spread; the click of the shuttle ceased, and the weavers rushed to their doors as the crowd tramped past.

Mr. Matthews led his men direct to the hotel—an establishment that was quite a curiosity in its way. Very different it was from the spacious and comfortable hotels to be found in the town nowadays. True, it was commodious; but it was low-roofed, the light was bad, and ventilation was worse. It stood in Greenwell Street, at the place now known as "the de'il's elbow." It was a rakish, skampish-looking building, yet it possessed a very grand name—"The Londonderry Hotel"—which name was coarsely painted upon a big board, together with the intimation that it provided entertainment for both man and beast.

The proprietor of this place was Andy Martin, a man possessed of remarkable cunning and shrewdness. No person could "do" Andy, but Andy, when so disposed, could "do" the sharpest of his customers. So notorious did he become in this respect that his name became a byword for over-reaching craft, and until this day the phrase is in common use; "Ye'll no come Andy Martin over me!" The man's nature was suspicion itself. He suspected every person of some design, and when he thought anyone with whom he was dealing meant to "do" him, his favourite expression was: "All in my eye!" That phrase, too, is a common one in Newtown and the Ards till now.

In the hotel of Andrew Martin the men were bountifully regaled with whiskey and beer, brown bread and cheese. When the hour of noon arrived, all were rested and refreshed. Mr. Matthews had issued his instructions as to the mode of procedure, so that when the men went forth into the street, each one knew the part he would be required to perform. By different routes they proceeded to the glen in which they had reason to believe Mr. M'Fadden was concealed and confined a prisoner.

Andy Martin had been informed of the business on hand, and he stood for some time looking after the motley crowd. Then, turning into the house, he saluted his wife with: "It's all in my eye, Betty Martin, to look for robbers' caves in the old Glen at Tullnagardy; it's all in my eye, Betty Martin."

Having so delivered his opinions, Andrew lit his pipe, and was very speedily enveloped in clouds of smoke.

No mill stood then where the Glen Mill rears its lofty chimney to-day. The place was wild and unfrequented. Dismounting, those who had horses left them at the end of the Glen, and proceeded on foot up the narrow and precipitous path. Their progress was slow, their movements cautious.

Where the concealed cave might lie they knew not.

They also dreaded lest they might be surprised by an ambuscade of the "Merry Hearts".

In many places the ground was wet and marshy; in others so overgrown with hazel, brambles and other underwood that every step was made with difficulty.

At length the entire party reached the great rock described in an earlier chapter. The men were, by this time, breathless and excited. Although not knowing the exact locality of the Smugglers' Cave something told them that they had reached the spot.*

* In a manuscript which the author has had the privilege of seeing, and which is at present lying before him, names of men who accompanied Mr. Matthews on this expedition are given. As they may prove

The pursuit now began to become eager and exciting. The party having divided themselves, each of the divisions followed up the branches of the stream. At one time they floundered over the large stones that covered the bed of the rivulet. At another they waded knee-deep in the waters of the mountain torrent. As they walked they cautiously raised the hanging plants and shrubs that might, by any possibility, cover the entrance to the cave.

In one of the divisions of the anxious seekers there was one master spirit. One form was ever at the front and untiring in his search.

It was Eddie. He had promised Miss M'Fadden in a few moments of brief conversation that he would certainly rescue her father. They were moments of bliss to Eddie. It was happiness to him unalloyed to look on the fair face of the lady and hear her calling him by name. Miss M'Fadden humoured the simple lad. She saw that he had conceived an ardent passion for her—his looks betrayed him.

The searchers had proceeded but a short way up the little river, when Eddie, more intrepid than the others, and being somewhat

---

interesting to some of our readers, we insert them as a note – Robert M'Cann, Innishargie; Patrick Johnston, Ballyeasborough; James Wilson, Kirkcubbin; Robert Coffey, Ballyeasborough; John Gray, Granshaw, Kirkcubbin; William Johnston, Ballyeasborough; Robert Black, Glastry; John Kennedy, Ballywalter; James M'Whirr, Kirkcubbin; Charles Patton, Ballyeasborough; Thomas Patton, Ballywalter; John Gibson, Ballyeasborough; Robert Murdock, Ballywalter; James Murdock, Ballywalter; John Patty, Kirkcubbin; Thomas Askin, Whitechurch; John Askin, Rureagh; John Taylor, Ballyeasborough; Henry Pyper, Kirkcubbin; Robert Maxwell, Ballywalter; William Shaw, Ballywalter; George Wilson, Kirkcubbin; Henry Taylor, Granshaw, Kirkcubbin; John Black, Ballyeasborough; Robert Connor, Glastry; John Aiken, Ballyeasborough; and William M'Minn, Whitechurch. "Besides these," the manuscript says, "there was a strange lad, who was called Eddie. His surname I do not remember to have heard."

in advance, started back and pointed to a spot in the high natural embankment. A network of underwood and hazels extended over the place.

The scouting parties now joined their forces and gathered round Eddie, looking towards the spot indicated.

"The cave is in there," he said, pointing with his finger. "When A lifted thae twigs an' things, A saw the hole, and the feet o' a lot o' fellows waitin' on us."

"They have been warned," said Mr. Matthews. "We must make haste, boys. Fifty pounds to the man who first gets out Mr. M'Fadden!"

There was a low but determined cheer from the men. In a body they approached the cave. The nature of the ground forbade a sudden rush. They stood still for a moment, irresolute.

"Starve them oot," said a voice.

"Na, na," said Eddie; "if they're warned there'll be mair here direkly."

"Burn them oot," said another.

"What will ye burn?" said a third big country fellow with a club; "wet * winna mak much o' a bleeze."

"No; but it'll make a smoke," said the doctor, who was now as eager as anyone to dislodge the robbers.

"But M'Fadden," said Matthews. "If we smoke or fire the cave, he will suffer, too!"

"De'il a fear, sir," said Eddie. "Mr. M'Fadden is in the cave inside. There's twa caves."

The arrangement was carried. It was determined to smoke them into submission.

A number of men now leaped up on the bank above where the cavern was situated. With their scythes they soon cleared away the brambles, grass and underwood. In a very few minutes the entrance

* A word(s), perhaps *whin*, seems to be missing here.

of the outer cave was exposed to view. The feet of several men were seen distinctly in the interior of it.

Mr. Matthews called upon them to surrender.

There was no answer returned from out the cavern. All was silence.

He again called upon them and warned them of their danger. But there was no reply.

"Well, take what you get," said he, and he turned and gave directions to the men.

Eddie, with all the excitement and energy of a half-witted nature, was vehement in his gesticulations, and planned.*

Men were dispatched to Newtown, and cans of turpentine and pitch were brought out to the Glen. A large fire was then kindled on the grass. In this, tow steeped in turpentine and pitch was lighted, and the burning, smoking masses thrown into the cave. The scene became most exciting. As the burning masses penetrated the cave they were hurled into the water or trampled out by those besieged.

Every instant it was expected that the robbers would submit, as the heavy clouds of black, filthy smoke rolled upwards. Eddie, perched on the opposite bank, apparently unconscious of danger, screamed and laughed with delight as the conspirators huddled further back into the cavern.

"Whun they gang intil the ither cave," said he, "A'll tell ye, boys, an' then ye can rush in!"

---

* This sentence is apparently incomplete, but no edition prior to Carswell's 1914 one was available against which to check it.

CHAPTER XXII

A Night of Horrors

WE must retrace our steps, once more, in order to preserve the chain of our narrative, and note the doings of other actors in our story.

The reader will remember that, in Chapter XIX., we described the fate which befell Commodore Bob at the hands of an infuriated populace, who strangled him upon the limb of a big tree that grew by the roadside near to the town of Kirkcubbin.

We now take the reader back to that revolting scene of rude justice and lynch law.

Swaying to and fro hung the body of Commodore Bob.

His clothes were in tatters; his limbs scratched and bleeding; his face swollen and black; his tongue protruding; his eyes, fixed in a stony stare, bursting from their sockets.

The sight was sickening; ay, even that maddened, excited crowd, now that the first fierce gust of passion had swept away, hung down their heads from a feeling of shame and remorse. The King of Terrors stood before them in hideous outline. They had deprived a fellow-being of his life; had taken the law into their own hands. Yea, they were murderers!

A sudden hush succeeded the storm of passion, and they turned, with a sense of loathing, to leave the unhallowed spot.

"What'll we dae wi' him?" cried one of the crowd.

That question, uttered suddenly, and in a loud tone of voice, dispelled the momentary gloom which had fallen upon the crowd, and a perfect hurricane of answers went forth.

"Cut him doon!"

"Bury him!"

"Let him hang there!"

"Let the craws eat him!"

"Burn the thief!"

These and other cries rent the air.

The leading spirits held the counsel. It was decided that the hideous object dangling from the tree would frighten women and children, not to speak of horses and cattle.

And so it was decided to cut the body down.

This was done. The huge limp form of the once active Commodore was flung, like that of a dog, by the common wayside.

And then came the question of how the body should be disposed of. It was unfit for the hallowed precincts of a graveyard; no farmer would permit the vile carcase to have a resting-place in his ground, so there remained but the King's highway as a burial place. Once again the crowd shouted and clamoured.

"He's no worth the bother!"

"Wha wud dig up the road for that vagabond!"

"Throw him intil some dyke sheugh!"

"Tak him tae Gunyin's mill and let the rats eat him."

The last proposal found instant favour with the lynchers, and elicited a ringing cheer, for by this time their qualms of conscience had subsided.

No sooner said than done, and eager hands seized upon the greasy rope that dangled from the Commodore's neck. Another moment, and those who held the rope started off at a brisk trot, dragging the body after them.

But, ere they had gone a dozen paces, several of the crowd interfered, and brought them to a stand.

"Dinnae pu' him efter ye like a dug!" remonstrated the big, kindly-looking farmer.

"An' what is he but a dug?" retorted one of the men who tugged at the rope, now slippery as an eel.

"He had a mither yince, like the rest o' us," said the first speaker, "an' he waznae aye a bad yin. Tak him tae the mill an' welkim, but dinnae trail him that wae."

"An' what'll we dae?"

"Carry him," said the farmer; "an A'll gie ye a lift."

The suggestion was agreed to. The rope was taken from the neck of the unfortunate man, and cut in two pieces of equal length. One portion was tightly bound round the Commodore's arms, the other round his legs. Then loops were made upon the ends of the ropes, and through these loops stout sticks were thrust—making a rough and impromptu bier. Two men at each side took hold of the ends of the sticks, and lifting the body from the ground they began the march to the old mill, changing hands occasionally by the way.

They had not far to go, a quarter of a mile or so brought them to their destination, the ruins of an old corn mill, long disused, and said to be literally alive with big, fierce, bold and hungry rats.

The body of the Commodore was dragged into the ruin, and flung upon the floor with many a rude jeer and blasphemous exclamation. There he was left to rot, or to furnish a meal for the filthy rats that infested the place, while the men who had killed him went their various ways, laughing and joking over their ghastly adventure.

....

It was the hour of midnight. The old mill stood like a grey spectre on the dreary common which stretched upon all sides, the grazing ground of stirks, near to the shore, and far from human habitation.

Hark! What sound is that?

Is it the cry of the seabird on its lonely flight?

No!

It comes from within the crumbling walls of the old mill, where a horrible sight is concealed by the thick black darkness of the night.

The Commodore lived!

"We are immortal till our work is accomplished," said a famous prince. The Commodore had apparently a mission yet to be fulfilled.

When cut down, he had presented every appearance of being dead. But, though reduced to a bloated, bleeding senseless mass, the vital spark had not fled. He lay for hours in the old mill, motionless—dead. Then slowly, very slowly—painfully, very painfully—consciousness returned. His heart beat; his pulses throbbed; his entire body was pervaded by a sharp, tingling sensation. Life had returned! But still he did not move; he uttered no sound. His mind was a complete blank—entire forgetfulness.

Then, with startling suddenness, reason regains her throne; the mental faculties resume their functions; memory awakens from its brief sleep of death. The Commodore starts, and utters a cry as though a knife had struck his heart—that cry that floated out upon the midnight air.

The doings of the previous day rise up before him with frightful and realistic distinctness. His murderous attack upon Willie Douglas; his robbery of the booty; his flight and capture—his execution!

Is he dead!

That is the question he asks himself. Darkness, thickness, envelopes him. His eyes are aching; his swollen tongue and his throat burn as though on fire and, trying to speak, his first words, choking and inarticulate, are:

"Water! For the love of God, water!"

He tries to rise, but feels that his arms and limbs are powerless. Are they dead? The horrible fancy seizes him that they are. But, no! He feels sensation of pain and numbness passing over them. Drawing up his knees and extending one of his stiffened hands towards them, he discovers, by the sense of touch, that a rope secures them together. He struggles to reach the knot, but cannot. And then the fact dawns upon him that his arms, too, are secured in some way, between his elbows and wrists, to his body.

Where is he? Shall he cry for help? Is he in a prison?

Have the "Merry Hearts" discovered his disloyalty, and confined him in a cave? Why did he not die outright?

Such are the questions that he asks mentally. And then, again and again, the horrors of his execution rise up before him, and he broods morbidly over the sensations which he had experienced. He feels the rope tightening round his neck, and a horrible sense of choking succeeds; he is hauled upward, kicking fiercely and instantly all is a blank—the blank of unconsciousness. He wakens again to life as his executioners lower him to earth and loosen the hempen rope. He pleads for mercy—the rope tightens—he chokes—he is hauled up—and again sensation ceases. Over and over again he recalls the phenomena of hanging, and feels convinced, as he does so, that death by strangulation is a painless one!

Hark! What is that?

He strains his ears and holds his breath.

Again that sound!

What is it?

A scratching and scampering as of kittens at play. A low, squeaking noise. A rushing and rustling sound. A small, cold object touches his hand. He utters a scream as shrill and piercing as that of a timid woman or a scared child, and struggles with all his determined strength to snap the ropes that bind him.

Rats?

At the sound of his voice they scamper off, squeaking with alarm, while the wretched man lies exhausted and quivering in every nerve. He loathes rats in his very soul: fears them with a horrible, superstitious fear, that cannot be allayed.

They come again, this time in troops. He sees their scintillant eyes flashing, like fiery sparks, in the darkness. He hears the rush of their bodies towards him, and the next moment they spring upon him, chasing each other as though in frolic. They swarm upon his breast, his head, his throat, with a suddenness that paralyses him. One of the loathsome creatures thrusts its cold nose between the Commodore's lips, startling him into such a frenzy of passion that he snaps at the beast suddenly and fiercely, biting the head clean from its body!

Spitting out the vile morsel he screams and kicks with all his might, and again the army of rats retreat.

Covered with huge beads of cold sweat, weak, sick, and full of unspeakable horror and disgust, the Commodore lay panting and exhausted. *Would they eat him alive?* He believed they would. All through his life he had regarded rats with a feeling of unaccountable repugnance. Here was the solution. His living body was to be their food. They would eat the flesh from off his bones, bit by bit, until he would bleed to death.

Oh, God, what a death to die!

Hush! What was that!

A sound of gnawing. It is quite close to him, or seems so, and he strains his ears to listen.

A soft, subdued sound as of teeth gnawing at a semi-hard and fibrous substance!

The Commodore moves not, for a dream of hope—a hope of life—darts into his breast and stills his wild alarm. He scarcely breathes. Not a muscle moves, so anxious does he feel.

For what?

For the rats to return! Some of them, attracted by the odour of the cart grease, are gnawing at the rope that binds him! If they all come—legions of them—he may soon be free! They crowd upon him, but he stirs not. They scramble and fight for a morsel of the dainty meal, and he is thrilled with wild joy as he feels the strands of the ropes rending, tearing, snapping, yielding, under the sharp teeth of his deliverers.

It is a period the duration of which he could not measure. Minutes or hours may have been that measure, but at last it was all over. One sudden effort of his arms and legs—an effort which might have been sooner made had not fear restrained him—and the last fibres of the ropes snapped like threads. The army of rats scampered off in terror, and the Commodore, giving vent to his feelings in a perfect yell of delight, sprang to his feet, saved from a horrible death; and, for the present at all events, free once more!

Next day, when some of the lynchers peeped cautiously into the mill, they had a sharp surprise. The man was gone! The ropes, too, had disappeared—not a vestige of them visible.

And the verdict arrived at was that the devil had carried off the body during the night. Till the present day, all through the broad Ards, the Commodore is spoken of as—"Bob the Devil."

CHAPTER XXIII

Commodore Bob Pays a Visit

THE Commodore was not long in making his way out of the mill, and into the open air. His sensations were of a mixed character, and his ideas were naturally somewhat confused. The scenes through which he had passed and the ordeals which he had endured were sufficient to unhinge minds very much stronger and better balanced than that possessed by smuggler Bob.

Having wandered aimlessly through the darkness for a dozen paces or so, his further progress was impeded by a hedge and ditch which barred his way. Here he sat down and tried to think.

The process was not an easy one; his mind was in a state of chaos. Gradually it cleared, however; and the Commodore, by the exercise of his strong will, forced himself to take a calm survey of his position, condition, and future prospects.

His position! Where was he? He could not tell. He had but a faint idea of the exact locality of the hanging scene. He knew that the lynchers attacked him upon the Kirkcubbin road, and not far from the town. But where was he now? How far had he been carried or driven?

But here his reflections were interrupted by a stamping and tramping of feet. Then a dark body dashed past him at a rapid trot—another, and another. In the darkness he failed to distinguish the outlines of the bodies. But his keen eyes discovered not far off what seemed to be a big moving mass of animals. Going down upon his knees he groped for a stone; and found one. This he flung towards the dark mass with all the force of which his strength was capable.

Instantly there was a wild stampede across the common, and the bellowing of cattle.

The Commodore smiled. He had found his bearings. He was upon Gunning's grazing ground. He had marked the spot upon a recent occasion, with a view to having a raid made upon the fine fat stirks that grazed there.

Theft, however, was not the question now. It was escape, and he must find the road.

"Trust to luck," was the Commodore's favourite maxim, and once more he committed himself to it. Keeping the ditch on the right hand he walked slowly forward, then suddenly stopped.

What does he hear?

He throws himself forward upon the ground, Indian fashion, and listens intently.

The sound which falls upon his ears is a grateful one. It is the roll and surge of the waters of Strangford Lough! Starting to his feet he faces the direction from which the sound comes, and steps out boldly. There is no further hesitation. Once upon the margin of the lough and he feels that he will be safe.

He pauses again, for he has reached the running stream. Never was there sweeter music than the wimpling of that liquid water. He literally flings himself into it, and laps the water greedily with his tongue, dog fashion. He feels as though he could drink that streamlet dry, but at length the cravings of thirst are satisfied, and he clambers up, refreshed and invigorated.

Half an hour later and he is upon the beach. The darkness is less dense now. Faint streaks of light are becoming visible in the far-off horizon, creeping slowly upward into the darkened heavens. On and on the Commodore journeys. His strength is failing him, and the pangs of hunger have succeeded the awful agony of his burning thirst.

"Trust to luck!" he mutters, clenches his teeth, and strides onward.

A gleam of light in the far distance, like a glimmering star!

The Commodore sees it, and hope once more fills his sinking

heart. It is a signal light from a cottage upon the shore, and the Commodore instantly divines its meaning. Far out to sea shoots the bright starlike gleam, telling the hardy smugglers that all is well, and the coast clear for the landing of their booty!

There is no uncertainty now about the Commodore's movements. With renewed strength he strides forward towards that beacon light. The tramp is long and wearisome to him in his present condition, but his strength of will overcomes his fatigue, and he is rewarded at last by seeing the dim outline of the house which he means to enter. He knows not nor cares not who may be the occupant, whether it be friend or foe. He is a hunted outlaw, and he must have the means of speedy flight.

In a lonely spot, close to the shore of Strangford Lough stood a wretched hovel, possessing but one inmate—Jack Rodgers. Jack had neither kith nor kin, and lived the life of a recluse. He had reached the age of seventy, but was still active, enjoyed excellent health, and looked like a man having fully twenty years before him.

In early life Jack had been a smuggler, taking part in many a deed of daring. Now, however, he had retired from active service; and, while to all appearance a penniless creature, rumour averred that he had amassed much of the current coin of the realm. In spirit he was a smuggler still; and, indeed, he was so in more than spirit. Near to his house the "Merry Hearts" had a landing-place and a cave, and when a landing during the night was contemplated Jack kept his signal light burning. In various other ways, too, he aided the "Merry Hearts," receiving in return a share of the spoil, or cash in lieu thereof.

On the night of the Commodore's adventure a landing was to be attempted. The revenue men had been decoyed away a distance of several miles upon a false scent, and so confident of success were the smugglers that it had not been considered necessary to keep the usual scout upon the shore.

Cowering over the smouldering ashes of a turf fire sat Jack Rodgers. Wonderfully acute were the old man's hearing and sight, but no sound seemed to reach him as he sat gazing from under his shaggy and grizzly eyebrows at the gleaming sparks in the heap of ashes before him.

Suddenly he started from his sitting posture and, darting to the window, extinguished the candle.

His quick ear had caught the sound of footsteps cautiously approaching, and he feared a surprise from the revenue officers.

A minute later and a hand tried the latch.

The door was barred and bolted.

"Apen the daur!" said a rough voice from without.

Jack was now behind the door, his ear pressed against the cracked timbers.

"Wha's there?" he asked.

"A friend—a "Merry Heart!" was the answer.

The voice sounded familiar to Jack, and he opened the door. The Commodore stepped in, and, closing the door, bolted and barred it with all the deftness of one accustomed to the work.

And so he was. His luck had once more served him, and he had stumbled upon one of the familiar haunts of the crew to which he belonged.

"Licht the cannel," he said, purposely disguising his voice.

Old Jack made his way to the hearth-stone, and lifting a piece of burning peat from the ashes speedily complied with the Commodore's order.

"Set it back there somewhaur, and darken the wundey," was the Commodore's command; and Jack obeyed without speaking a word.

Then, for the first time, Jack turned to survey his visitor. At first he did not recognise the Commodore, and the sight of the rags and tatters which formed his only covering sent the old fellow into a fit of convulsive laughter.

"What the h—l ir ye lauchin' at?" growled the Commodore fiercely, and this time in his natural voice.

Jack's jaw fell, and his laughter ceased with startling suddenness. He stood staring at the man before him in speechless wonder, and with a look of absolute horror upon his face. The Commodore appeared to enjoy the old man's surprise, and stood silent and grinning.

"The Commodore, A declare tae God!" at length was the utterance of Jack, as he sat down upon his stool, fairly overcome with the appearance of one whom he had thought dead, for the lynching of the Commodore had been reported far and wide, and even old Jack had heard the thrilling story.

"What ir ye glowerin' at?" asked the Commodore. "A buddy wud think ye had seen a ghaist."

"An' that's jest what A think A see—Guid save me!" stammered the old fellow.

The Commodore stepped nearer to Jack, the old map shrinking back as he did so.

"Dinnae be scaured," said the Commodore, in a softer tone. "A'm alive, Jack, but deein' wi' hunger. Get me sumthin' tae eat. Hurry yersel'!"

But Jack still sat staring in gaping wonder.

"Dae ye feel that?" cried the Commodore, bringing his hand down with a slap upon Jack's shoulder. "Is that like a ghaist's hand?"

"Na," was the answer; "but A cannae beleev my een. A heerd ye wur deid, that the folk—"

"Never min' what ye heerd," said the Commodore, his surly manner returning. "Get me whatever meat ye hae in the hoose and A'll shew ye then hoo a ghaist can eat. Hurry yersel', A say!"

Jack delayed no longer. He dragged an old round table into the centre of the kitchen, and placed beside it an old rope-bottomed chair, upon which the Commodore sat down. Then he brought from a cupboard some home-made bread and a piece of boiled bacon. These he placed before his guest, who, seizing the lump of bacon between his two hands, attacked it with his teeth savagely, like a hungry wolf.

Jack looked on in silence, half amused now that his fright was passing off, and it was fully five minutes before the Commodore uttered a word. Then he asked:

"Hae ye ony whusky?"

"Of course," said Jack, going back to his cupboard, and returning with a big black bottle, which the Commodore seized upon with rude haste, and, placing it to his lips, gulped of the contents greedily.

"Ah!" he gasped, as he put down the bottle, and wiped his mouth, "A cud guess whaur ye got that frae, Jack."

"A daur say ye cud."

Once more the victuals were attacked by the half-famished man, who tore off huge pieces of bread and meat which he bolted with but little mastication, and it did seem as though he never would be satisfied.

But he did stop at last!

Another long, eager pull at the black bottle, and then the Commodore motioned to Jack, who had still remained standing, to take a seat.

Jack sat down.

"Len' me your pipe," said the Commodore.

Jack handed the pipe over, in silence, and then regarded his unwelcome visitor with a steady stare in which fear and horror were combined.

Did some mysterious monitor whisper in his ear a warning word of what was about to happen?

CHAPTER XXIV

Dead Men Tell no Tales

FOR fully a quarter of an hour the Commodore sat smoking in silence. Then he laid down the pipe upon the table, and addressing old Jack, said:

"Ye expect the boys the nicht?"

"A dae," said Jack.

"What ir they bringin'?"

"A dinnae ken."

"Did ye no hear ocht?"

"They spauk aboot tabacca."

Another brief space of silence intervened, and then the Commodore remarked, with a grin:

"So ye thocht a wuz deid."

"Ay, A shairly did, an' so diz the hale country."

"Weel, Jack, the man that's born tae be hung wull never be aither drooned or shot, an' A suppose that auld sayin' cuts baith roads."

"Mebbe it diz," said Jack, "an' mebbe—"

He paused, as though unwilling to finish the sentence.

"Mebbe what?" growled the Commodore.

Jack did not answer.

"What wuz ye gaun tae say?" queried the Commodore, roughly.

"A wuz gaun till say that mebbe it wad be weel ye had been deid," stammered Jack.

Jack remained silent, and the look in his face puzzled the Commodore, who, in an excited tone of voice, demanded an explanation.

"Weel, if A maun tell ye, A maun," said Jack.

"A wheen o' the boys were here last night talkin' aboot ye."

"What did they say?"

"That if ye had got intil their hands it wudnae been hangin' ye wud a got."

"What wud it a been?"

"Oh, yin said yin thing, an' anither said anither. Sum said they wud a roasted ye alive; ithers said they wud a drooned ye in a sack; and ithers said they wud a cut yer tongue oot o' yer heid an' rammed it doon yer throat."

"What fur, d—n them!" growled the Commodore.

"Didn't ye rob Wullie Douglas o' five hunner poun', an' then knock his brains out at the roadside?" hissed old Jack from between his teeth. The man's courage had returned now; and, as he spoke, his eyes flashed from beneath their shaggy brows.

"An' what did *you* say?" asked the Commodore.

"A said it wud serve ye richt."

An evil light gleamed in the eyes of the Commodore.

"When dae ye expect the boys?" he asked.

"They'll no land when they see the place in darkness; A maun pit the cannel back in the wundey," said Jack starting to his feet.

"Na, ye'll dae naethin' o' the soart," growled the Commodore. "Ye'll pit nae licht there till A'm oot o' this."

"Then the suiner ye're oot o' this the better," said Jack, snappishly.

"Why?"

"Acause if ony o' the boys cums in, there micht be rough wark. A'm gaun tae pit the cannel in the wundey noo."

"Ye'll wait a bit," said the Commodore.

"Na, no anither minit," said Jack. And so saying he lifted the candle to replace it against the window pane.

In an instant the Commodore was at his side.

"Pit doon that cannel!" he said.

Jack turned to face the Commodore, and as he did so, the tiger-like glance of the eyes which looked into his awed him.

He put down the candle, muttering as he did so:

"Gang awa'! Gang awa'!"

"A hae somethin' tae say till ye first," said the Commodore.

"What is it?"

"Ye'll no tell the boys that A wuz here."

"A'll no promise that," said Jack.

"Ay, but ye wull."

The Commodore's voice was hard; its tone determined.

"Dae ye hear me?" hissed the Commodore.

Jack made no reply.

"Dae ye hear me?" hissed the Commodore.

"A dae."

"Promise!"

"Na."

"By God ye wull! Sit doon!" and as the Commodore spoke he caught Jack by the shoulders, forcing him down violently upon a chair.

Jack was now thoroughly alarmed. And well he might be, for the blood of the Commodore was up, and there was murder in his eye.

"A'll promise!" gasped Jack.

But the Commodore replied not. The time for parley had passed, and his mind was made up that Jack should have no chance of betraying him and setting the bloodhounds upon his track. Seizing the old man by the neck, with both hands, he lifted him bodily from the chair and flung him savagely at his feet. His body struck the damp earthen floor with a dull sickening thud.

Quick as lightning the Commodore dropped heavily upon his knees upon Jack's breast, and seized him by the throat.

The unfortunate creature struggled, and strove to speak, but in vain. His face grew black. His tongue protruded from his mouth; but still that vice-like grip relaxed not. The Commodore seemed to gloat upon the contorted features, the starting eyeballs, the swollen and protruding tongue—all rendered doubly horrible in the dim and flickering light of the tallow candle. With his left hand he seized Jack's tongue and, fastening his nails upon it, dragged it out to its utmost limits. Then, loosing his grip upon the throat with his right hand, he lifted a knife that lay upon the table and began deliberately to cut the man's tongue out by the very root!

The knife was blunt. Jacks struggles were fearful; the snorting, gurgling sounds he uttered were horrible. But the Commodore hacked and sawed, with cool deliberation, until the tongue came away, a bleeding lump of flesh in his hand.

And then he rose, leaving his victim rolling and writhing upon the floor in unspeakable agonies.

The Commodore laid the bleeding tongue upon the plate from which he had eaten; wiped his hands upon an old towel which hung upon a nail; and then, without a word, undid the fastenings of the door, and walked out calmly and quietly as though nothing had occurred.

Next morning, when a neighbour called, he found old Jack lying cold, and stark, and stiff, and dead.

An alarm was given, and the people flocked in to see the awful sight. One discovery shocked them more than all the rest. Jack, in his dying moments, had struggled to his feet and obtained a piece of chalk, with which he had been in the habit of making marks, as a memoranda, upon the framework of the door or window. And then, falling or lying down again to die, he had traced with the chalk upon the damp, brown, earthen floor, in shaky but legible characters, the words:

"Commodore Bob."

CHAPTER XXV

The Revenue Cutter

TWO days after the events narrated in the preceding chapter, His Majesty's revenue cutter *Dart* lay off Greypoint, about midway between that rocky promontory and the Carrickfergus shore.

On the deck stood her commander, Captain Nelson; engaged, as he had been for some time, looking through his glass at an object upon the water which was invisible to the naked eye.

Lowering his glass at length, he addressed a smart-looking lad who had been hovering near and watching him, with:

"Here, my boy, take the glass, and see what you can make of that."

"Ay, ay, sir," cried the lad, promptly taking hold of the glass and darting up the rigging with the nimbleness of a squirrel.

Sweeping the glass along the shore, upon the County Down side, the boy at length brought it to bear upon what looked like a seagull skimming the surface of the blue waters. This he watched closely until from the deck the shout came up to him:

"Do you hear aloft?"

"Ay, ay, sir!"

"What do you make of it?"

"A hooker, sir; flying a signal. One man aboard."

"Stay where you are and keep your eyes upon her," sang out the captain.

"Ay, ay, sir!" and the boy resumed his watch.

"Mr. Elliott," said Captain Nelson, addressing his mate, who had just joined him, "I fancy somehow that fellow wants to board us. He may bring us news."

"Quite possible," replied the mate.

"How now, my lad?" cried the Captain, looking aloft. "How's she heading?"

"Right upon us, sir."

"What's she like?"

"A smallish craft, with every rag she can stretch to it."

"You may come down."

The lad descended, and returned the glass to the captain, who, raising it to his eyes and bringing it to bear upon the strange craft, stood for several minutes without speaking.

Then, handing his glass to the mate, he said:

"Have an eye on her, Mr. Elliott; I am going to my cabin to write some letters. If I am wanted, call me."

The boy aloft had accurately described the craft, which was now fully within the mate's range of vision. She was evidently of the "hooker" class, and steering for the cutter. On she came, at a spanking rate, right before the wind, and the worthy mate, putting aside the glass, awaited the approach of the probable visitor.

It was a visitor, and very soon within hail was one of the Strangford Lough fishing craft, carrying two sails—a mainsail and a foresail, the latter worked by long ropes leading aft, and the former traversing on a bent-iron bar across the stern over the rudder—easily managed by one hand.

"Boat ahoy!" sang out the mate, as the sails of the hooker were hauled down, and the broad-beamed clumsily-built boat glided up alongside of the revenue cutter.

By this time the entire crew, twenty in number, were on deck, leaning over the side of the *Dart*, and gazing curiously at the stranger. When the occupant of the boat came in full view, a perfect shout of laughter went up from the cruisers.

And little wonder.

The boatman was clothed—if the word can be so applied—in tatters. His eyes were both blackened, his face bore some ugly cuts and bruises, his half-naked legs and arms were covered with wounds and scratches.

"Shiver my timbers, but here's a fish!" bawled a sturdy seaman, as he flung him a rope by which to secure his boat.

Amid laughter, shouting and jeering, the man was hoisted upon deck, where he stood, for a moment, regarding the sailors with a sullen stare.

"Where is the captain?" he demanded.

"In his cabin," said the mate. "Pray, what is your business?"

"A'll tell him that when A see him," was the sullen reply.

"Then come this way," said the good-natured mate, leading the way to the captain's cabin, and followed closely by the man whose name the reader has probably guessed—Commodore Bob!

The mate knocked at the captain's door, and his knock was answered by:

"Come in!"

"This man has just come aboard, sir," said the mate, "and says he wishes to speak with you."

Having thus introduced the Commodore, Mr. Elliott retired.

The captain tugged at his iron-grey moustache in his efforts to conceal an amused smile as he gazed upon the ragged individual who stood before him.

"Well, my man," he said at last; "is there anything that I can do for you?"

"A mebbe can dae sumthin' for you, sir," answered the Commodore, pulling his forelock with an awkward attempt to appear civil.

"And what is that, my man?"

"Wad ye like tae catch a smuggler?" queried the Commodore, with a familiar grin, and quietly taking a seat.

"Yes," said the captain; "I shouldn't have the slightest objection. Where is he?"

"Oh, ye maun wait till I shew ye," was the Commodore's answer, accompanied by another grin.

"What is your name?" enquired the captain.

"Oh, niver min' my name; that'll mak nae odds," replied the Commodore, evasively.

"Well, where do you come from?"

"Frae the County Doon side."

"That's a very wide answer, my man."

"Well, A cum frae Strangford Lough."

"Ah, that's more definite," said the captain, beginning to feel interested. You're a 'Merry Heart,' I suppose, eh?"

"Weel, mebbe A em, an' mebbe A em not, sir."

"Never mind," said the captain, smiling; "what do you propose to say to me? What is the business which you came to talk to me about?"

The Commodore rubbed his hands together, clasped them across his knees, and looking keenly at the captain, asked:

"Ir ye wullin' tae pye me?"

"Certainly"

"Hoo much?"

"That depends."

"On what?"

"Upon the nature and value of your services."

"A see," said the Commodore, and then he lapsed into silence, as though uncertain what to say next.

The captain was becoming impatient.

"Let me hear what you can do, and what you expect by way of reward."

Thus brought to the point, the Commodore unbosomed himself.

He told how a valuable cargo of smuggled goods was seen to be brought from the Isle of Man and concealed at a convenient hiding-place prior to removal to Pirrie's Castle.* He told how he

* Pirrie's Castle, now known as "Little Clandeboye" was a famous place

was familiar with all the hiding-places of the "Merry Hearts," and that he could betray the whole gang into the hands of the Government. All this he said he could and would do provided he were suitably rewarded.

Captain Nelson listened attentively, never once interrupting his visitor, but eagerly drinking in every word he uttered.

When, at length, the Commodore paused, Captain Nelson enquired, in an apparently careless tone:

"How much do you want?"

"Five humner!"

The captain laughed.

"Five hundred *what?"* he asked.

"Guineas!" said the Commodore; with blunt emphasis.

"Well, we shall see," replied the captain, touching a bell as he spoke.

The mate appeared almost instantly in answer to the summons.

"Mr. Elliott," said the captain, "take this man on deck, and see that he gets something to eat and drink."

"Yes, sir. Anything else, sir?"

"Yes; get him a change of clothing, and see that he is made comfortable."

"Yes, sir."

The mate turned to go, beckoning to the Commodore to follow. The Captain stopped him, saying:

"By the way, cast his boat adrift, and see that he does not leave this ship. If he attempts to leave, put him in irons."

The Commodore's jaw fell, and the look which came upon his face was sufficient to draw a smile from the gallant captain of the smart cruiser *Dart.*

---

in the smuggling days of which we write. Till this day may be seen there the huge underground caverns in which goods were stored until they could be disposed of in Belfast or other places.

CHAPTER XXVI

A Chase

THE mate of the *Dart* allowed the Commodore no time for remonstration with Captain Nelson, but promptly turned him out of the cabin and hurried him forward to the men's quarters, where he at once communicated the captain's orders.

Two hours later, and the Commodore would not have been recognised by his closest acquaintance. His hair had been cut, his beard shaven off, his tattered garments had been replaced by a suit of seamen's clothes.

Captain Nelson having sent for the Commodore, with a view to further questioning him, was positively startled by the man's changed appearance.

"Well, my bold 'Merry Heart'," he exclaimed, cheerily, "how do you like your change of quarters?"

"No terble weel, Captain."

"And why?"

"Acause A dinnae want tae be here."

"Then why did you come here?"

"Tae gie ye information."

"You didn't give much, my man."

"A think A gied ye a' that was needid."

"Well, Mr. Merry Heart, I think differently. Your story may be true or it may be false. To be candid with you, I don't think it would cost you a very great effort to tell a big lie, especially if you wanted to play a practical joke upon one of the King's revenue cruisers; and therefore I mean to keep you here for the present.

"Hoo lang, Captain?"

"That depends upon circumstances. So long as you behave properly you shall be well treated. Stay on deck, keep a sharp lookout for your smuggling friends, and give the word when you sight them. Then leave the rest to me. You may go now."

That day passed, and nothing worthy of note occurred. The night was black and squally, and the following morning augured a gale. Acting upon the Commodore's advice, sail had been made, and the *Dart* was now lying off Ballyhalbert, and well out to sea. Under small head-sail, the large main continually luffing her to the wind, so deadened her way, from the rudder being almost across to counteract it, that she barely went two knots an hour through the water; and neither gaff topsail nor jib being visible, it was scarcely possible at a distance to distinguish her from a large hooker. Thus until afternoon did the *Dart* keep watch over the approaches to the County Down coast.

Captain Nelson was growing impatient, and more than ever suspected the Commodore of having deceived him. Turning to the Commodore, who, holding on to the main shrouds, was looking outwards in the teeth of the blast, now blowing fiercely, he said:

"It strikes me your friends have given us the slip."

"A wudnae be surprised," was the sullen reply. "But A see a sail noo."

"Where?" cried the Captain.

"There!" said the Commodore, pointing to a small white object only just visible.

"Sail ho!" came from the look-out aloft; and the Captain, handing his glass to the Commodore, directed him to have a look at the sail in sight.

Adjusting the glass, the Commodore watched for fully a minute, and then, lowering the glass, said quietly:

"It's the *Betty*, a smuggler schooner, an' she's heading for Ballyquintin Point."

Preparations for a chase were instantly made, and the cutter, bearing all possible, fairly flew through the water.

"Load the guns!" shouted the Captain. "We may want to throw a shot after him."

"Ye hae yer match afore ye noo," said the Commodore, addressing the Captain.

"How does she sail?" enquired the Captain.

"Like the win' itsel'," was the answer; "there's naethin' in the Lough can bate her!"

....

The reader will recollect the brief description given, in the third chapter of this story, of the individual who presided at the initiation of Willie Douglas into the "Merry Hearts' Association," and who was addressed by all the members as "Captain." The reader will now renew that gentleman's acquaintance by stepping on board the *Betty* as she scuds along the dangerous coast stretching from Ballyhalbert to the entrance of Strangford Lough, or Strangford Bar.

The *Betty* had not an inviting or tidy appearance. She looked a very dirty craft, very like a well-grimed collier, on which paint and cleanliness seemed never to have been expended. But appearances are not always to be relied upon. The *Betty*, though dirty externally, was a very tidy boat within, and one of the fastest clippers of her day. Her skipper, Captain Jenkins, was a fearless sailor. He knew every inch of the coast, and was largely engaged in the contraband trade. He had discovered the presence of the *Dart* long before his own vessel had been sighted, and he felt pretty certain that she was not in the place without having received some positive information. He had contemplated a landing in the neighbourhood, but that was now impossible. His only chance now lay in showing his heels and making round for Strangford Lough in the hope of outrunning the cutter. To this, then, he bent every energy of his strong mind and soon the *Betty* was spinning along under every inch of canvas she could spread.

"Now," he chuckled, "if that fellow only takes an hour's doze, we'll shew him fun. Ease her, Bill; ease her, man—so, not too near, or the back swag will take a stick out of her. Here, you boy, up with you; make yourself snug aloft, and keep your eye on that chap, or I'll rope's end you!"

"Ay, ay, sir;" and the lad went up the rigging in a trice.

"Do you want a glass aloft there?" shouted the Captain.

"Better pass one up, sir," said the boy, "we're leaving him fast."

The *Betty* went tearing along at a rate which, if continued, would soon place her in safety; and the Captain, telescope in hand, kept looking ahead.

"Halloa!"

The shout came from the boy aloft.

"He's at somethin'. Up goes his gafftopsail and jib; he's after us, sir," shouted the lad.

CHAPTER XXVII

Daft Eddie's Fate

WE must now retrace our steps to the smugglers' cave in the Glen of Tullynagardy.

It will be remembered that in chapter XXI. the men from Ballyeasborough and other places had discovered the entrance to the hiding-place in which it was supposed Mr. M'Fadden had been imprisoned by the "Merry Hearts," pending the arrival of the £500 for which Willie Douglas had been dispatched.

As already described, an effort was being made to smoke out the occupants of the cave, and Daft Eddie, perched upon the opposite bank, had shouted:

"Whun they gang intil the tither cave" (meaning an inner chamber of which Eddie appeared to have some knowledge) "A'll tell ye, boys, an' then ye can rush in."

Scarcely had the lad uttered these words than from the mouth of the cave there issued a small stream of white smoke.

And then the report of a gun echoed through that wild and lonely glen.

Eddie started up convulsively, waved his arms wildly in the air, and, toppling over, rolled down the bank into the water.

The spectators uttered a yell of rage, and frenzied passion now assumed the place of cool reason. Caution and discretion were banished by the mad desire for vengeance. Shots were fired into the cave at random, while Eddie, under cover of the firing, was carried to the rear and placed in charge of the doctor.

At last the unequal contest ended, and the occupants of the cave surrendered. They were dragged out into the open air more dead than alive.

Then Matthews and his men rushed into the cavern to rescue the prisoner.

The cave was bare and empty!

Choking and half-blinded-by the smoke, Mr. Matthews hurried out of the cave.

"Not there!" he exclaimed, addressing his men. "Not there! All our trouble in vain, and poor Eddie killed!"

Wringing his hands in an agony of despair, he sought the spot to which Eddie had been carried, and where he now lay upon the grass.

The boy heard the words, and, opening his eyes, recognised Mr. Matthews, who knelt down beside him, and took his hand.

Eddie smiled sadly, and then, in a voice which was low and weak, said:

"He's no there; he's in the cave that's inside. There's a spring, if ye can fin' it, that'll mak the daur flee apen."

"Oh, we'll get our friend before long," said Mr. Matthews, trying to cheer the lad. "Are you much hurt?"

"A'm beginnin' tae feel it badly noo, sir," said Eddie. And he closed his eyes as if to go to sleep.

Mr. Matthews returned to the cavern. He looked anxiously around him for some trace of bolts or springs. In this also he was disappointed.

"If ye wud let a wheen o' us at it wi' the crowbars, sir," said one of the men, "A'll warran' ye we'll pit the wall doon."

No sooner suggested than the plan was adopted.

All the crowbars among the party were called into requisition. The men worked by relays. In a few minutes the cave was being wonderfully enlarged.

"Hush, boys: stop, for the love of God!" said one of the men, pausing in his work.

All were silent and listened intently.

"There's a voice speaking in this way, sir," said the man who had called silence.

Mr. Matthews came forward to the place and listened.

"Who are you, or what do you want?" said a voice from the inside, behind the rock upon which the men had been engaged.

"It's the maister's voice," said two to three in a breath.

"M'Fadden, are you there?" roared Mr. Matthews.

"Yes; is that you, Matthews?" came forth from the bowels of the earth.

"Yes; all right! Now, give way, boys; we'll ruin their cave for them, at all events."

The men wrought with heartiness and energy, but the solid rock was strong. For fully a quarter of an hour it resisted all their efforts. At last a seam or crack in the rock was exposed to view. Into this crevice the men inserted the points of their crowbars.

"Now, boys, pull together—whoop!"

There was an awful crash, then a roar like thunder. The men tumbled and rolled over each other as the ponderous door yielded to their energy and swung open unexpectedly.

Mr. M'Fadden walked forth from his tomb more like a ghost than a living creature.

After the long incarceration in the dark dungeon, the light of day blinded him. His limbs were weak for want of exercise. He staggered forward amid a ringing cheer from all who stood around. Even Eddie on his grassy couch could scarcely refrain from a shout of welcome and of joy.

The old friends grasped each other's hands and tears stood in the eyes of Mr. Matthews as his old friend stood before him, squalid, grizzled, and in rags. His cheeks were withered and shrivelled. His eyes were sunken and hollow; and the glare of heaven's daylight caused them to shrink up and almost disappear.

"My daughter!"—they were the first words uttered by the old man.

"All safe, and waiting for you."

"I thank thee, God, my child is safe," said he, reverently. Then turning to Mr. Matthews asked where she was.

"With us in Newtown."

"In Newtown! Where am I?"

"Within a mile of Newtown."

"My God, I thought we were on the Killinchy side of Lough Cowan. We certainly went by boat, and I was kept a prisoner near Killinchy. I was brought to this place blindfold and on horseback."

Having thus gained the first particulars of the events which had befallen them since the fatal night in which the house at Ballyeasborough was consumed by fire, the two old friends proceeded towards the town.

Vast crowds of people had gathered at the head of William Street to meet the procession coming home. The good people of Newtown were perfectly ignorant that a cave had existed in their neighbourhood. The news, therefore, spread like wildfire. They watched with the keenest interest the result of the exploration. Rumour, with her hundred tongues, had blazed the report through the town that a robbers' cave had been discovered in the Glen, and that a party of men from the low country had gone out to fight them. The crowd was consequently large and excited.

CHAPTER XXVIII

The Golden Bowl is Broken

THE procession, as it moved on towards the town, received a perfect ovation from the warm loyal hearts that always lived in Newtown.

Mr. Matthews and Mr. M'Fadden were at the front. Then followed the prisoners who had tried to defend cave. They were all miners, and, as it happened, evil-disposed Welshmen. They were closely guarded by the stout yeomen of the Ards around whom thronged the eager populace with jeers and shouts and curses on the miners. Poor Eddie, stretched upon a door and borne by four stalwart men, brought up the rear.

Shortly after his arrival at the hotel in Greenwell Street, he insisted on going home to his loved island of Mahee, so full of legendary and historic reminiscences. The doctor, knowing that this case was beyond his skill and that the end was rapidly approaching, humoured him.

A hammock was slung between two horses, and in this way Eddie reached the green shores of Killinchy again, round which his early days were spent.

His mind, weak and wandering as it was, clung with wonderful tenacity to his old loved haunts. In his dreams he sailed over the blue waters of Lough Cowan and gazed far down into its pebbly depths, noting the sea-shells and the tangle. He visited once more in the fitful wanderings of his fever the many islands that stud the placid bosom of the lough. In his dreams he again wandered over the sunny slopes of ancient Turneykill, or the grassy nooks he knew so well on Calf Island, Rainish and Sketrick. Again his dream would change, and the name of Martha hovered o'er his lips. His love for Miss M'Fadden was great, and all the greater that it was concealed. Although with the natural instinct of woman she may have guessed how lay the poor daft boy's affections, she never knew it till he was gone. Day by day his frame grew weaker and his eyes grew brighter, and his voice still lower. Medical skill did all for him that medical skill could do, for Mr. M'Fadden saw to that. But it was all in vain.

The pitcher had been shattered at the well. The golden bowl was broken, and the silver cord was fast becoming loosed.

If was a bright, warm day in early summer, and the pale lad lay adying. Eccentric in all his life, he was peculiar in his death. His friends anxiously stood around him, for they knew the hour was near.

"Mother," he said, "I'm goin' tae Martha. She called me Eddie, an' I called her Martha yince. Place me in my little boat, Mother, for I maun go. I will give her my fishing rod as a present, Mother; but com' quickly—place me in my boat—"

The silver cord was loosed. He had sailed away from earth. The poor innocent, ill-used lad, that found neither home nor name in the world, left it peacefully to find a home in heaven.

He was buried in the old churchyard of Tullynakill (or, as it was called, Turneykill), and many mourners were present at his funeral, for with whom was "Daft Eddie of Killinchy" not a favourite? Old and young, rich and poor, were accustomed to his strange manner, and loved him all the more.

There was a headstone mysteriously erected to his memory in the churchyard over his grave. It bore no name, no date—nothing but the plain word, "Eddie." No one knew how it was erected; no one knew by whom. He was a child of love—and all his epitaph was one small word—the name he best was known by, written in that plain granite slab, that still invites the attention of the tourist in the quiet churchyard of Tullynakill, which overlooks the waters of the Lough.

CHAPTER XXIX

The End of the Chase

LET us now return to the smuggler craft being hotly pursued by the revenue cutter.

The lad who kept watch aloft had announced skipper:

"He's at something. Up goes his gafftopsail and jib. He's after us, sir!"

"Keep your eye on him," shouted the captain. "Luff, Bill, luff; get a pull on the sheets, boys."

The entire hands were on deck, and the captain thus addressed them:

"Boys, many a run we have had together, and I hope we'll have lots more in days to come. I must, however, tell you what you probably see for yourselves—that we are just now in danger. That vessel should she come within range of us will try to sink us. Our only chance is to round Ballyquintin Point. Once in Strangford Lough we are safe, but not till then. Let every man do his best."

There was a hearty cheer in response.

Every man's face wore a look of grim determination, a look that meant death rather than capture or defeat.

And the *Betty*—what of her? Like a thing of life she flew over the waves, sending the white spray dashing from her bows, and answering to the helm splendidly.

"Bill, she works beautifully," said the captain, addressing the steersman.

"Ay, ay, sir; that she does; and it wants a smart fellow to catch her," was the cheery answer.

....

With a stormy wind abaft the beam, the *Dart* had every prospect of speedily coming up with the chase. The wind was momentarily gaining strength, and Captain Nelson's face wore an anxious look.

"I don't half like this," he said, addressing Mr. Elliott. "It's an ugly coast this, and that fellow knows it much better than we do. We'll have to take in a reef. Forward there! Do you make him out now?"

"Right ahead, sir, right ahead," answered the lookout.

"Don't lose him, then; these fellows are up to every dodge."

Captain Nelson had cause for anxiety. The wind had veered round to the south-east; there was an ebb-tide, and any attempt to cross Strangford bar must be attended with infinite danger. Yet still the chase went on. A gun was fired, another, and another, from the bows of the *Dart*, but the iron messengers fell harmless in the water, and the captain of the *Betty* laughed defiance at the summons.

The *Betty*, piloted by skilful hands, had safely rounded Ballyquintin Point, the *Dart* ebbing fully a couple of miles astern. Elliott, the mate, ventured a word of remonstrance with Captain Nelson. He pointed the dangerous nature of the coast, the almost utter hopelessness of the pursuit, the probability of again meeting the chase in open waters and capturing her. But the captain had made up his mind to follow, be the peril what it might.

The end was near. Ignorant of the extent of Ballyquintin reef, the steersman guided the *Dart* over its extreme point, which lay fully seventeen feet under water. A mighty billow caught the vessel, bearing her aloft for a brief second, and then, breaking by the nature of the reef, the *Dart* seemed descending to the very centre of the earth. Then, swift as thought, came a following billow, pouring its green flood over the weather quarter and sweeping all before it.

"She's on the reef!" was the wild cry of the crew, as the gallant ship, helpless as an infant in the clutch of the waves, was lifted and hurled against the black rocks beneath. The *Dart* was literally smashed to pieces, and her crew precipitated amongst the waves, their shrieks smothered by the tempest's howl. One man alone was saved to tell the tale. He caught upon a floating spar, to which he lashed himself and was, after the lapse of hours, washed ashore.

The incident aroused the ire of the Government, and the measures which they adopted were so stringent that the "Merry Hearts" became utterly disorganised. Their doings, or a part of them, have here been recorded and now our story ends.

The men captured at the Tullynagardy cave were sentenced to transportation for life. A descendant of Captain Nelson still lives at Portaferry, and a fine manly fellow he is, the owner of several stout fishing and sailing boats that ply the waters of Strangford Lough.

All the actors in our story have long since passed away. Willie Douglas, restored to his faithful wife, devoted himself to farming, and lived a quiet, uneventful life. Mr M'Fadden died at a ripe old age, and not until grandchildren prattled upon his knees. Some of his remoter relatives are living in the Ards till the present day.

THE END.

GLOSSARY

A	I
a	have
a'	all
aboon	above
aboot	about
acause	because
accause	because
aff	off
afore	before
agen	again, against
ain	own
airt	part, area
aither	either
an'	and
ane	one
anither	another
apen	open
areaddy	already
a'thegither	altogether
athoot	without
auld	old
ava	at all
awa, awa'	away
awfu'	awful
ax	ask
ay	yes
aye	always
baith	both

bate	beat
beleev	believe
bizness	business
bleeze	blaze
blethers	nonsense
blin'faul	blindfold
blissin'	blessing
bonnie	fine
boun'	bound
brae	hill
buddie	person
cam	came
canna	can't
cannae	can't
cannel	candle
carle	man
caul'	cold
cauld	cold
chiel	child
claes	clothes
coont	count
cove	fellow
craws	crows
creesh	grease
cud	could
cum	come
cummed	came
dae	do
daein'	doing
daith	death
daur	dare
daur	door

daurnae	daren't
dayli'go(n)	dusk
deein'	dying
deevils	devils
deid	dead
de'il	devil
didnae	didn't
din	done
dinnae	don't
direkly	directly
div	do
diz	does
dizn't	doesn't
dochter	daughter
doo	dove
doobled	doubled
doon	down
doot	doubt
dra'	draw
drap	drop
drookit	drenched
drooned	drowned
duds	clothes
dug	dog
een	eyes
efter	after
em	am
eneuch	enough
enuch	enough
faither	father
farder	farther
fause	false

feered	afraid
fin'	find
flee	fly
forgie	forgive
fowk	folk
frae	from
frichtened	frightened
friens	friends
fu'	full
fun	found
fur	for
gang	go
gaun	go, going
ghaist	ghost
gie	give
gied	gave
gin	by, when
gin	if
glowerin'	looking, staring
gowd	gold
gruppin'	gripping
Guid	God
guid	good
hae	have
hain't	haven't
hale	whole
hame	home
han'	hand
haud	hold
heerd	heard
heid	head
herm	harm

herricane	hurricane
hert	heart
heth	faith
hev	have
honner	honour
hoose	house
hunner	hundred
'il	will
intil	into
ir	are
ither	other
iver	ever
jab	job
jest	just
jist	just
ken	know
kens	knows
ketched	caught
kimmer	wife
knowe	hillock
kroobin	crab
kureosity	curiosity
laddie	boy
lang	long
lauchin'	laughing
lavin'	leaving
leddies	ladies
leddy	lady
len'	lend
licht	light

lock	lot
loss	lose
lukin'	looking
mac'rel	mackerel
mair	more
maister	master
mak	make
maun	man
maun	must
mebbe	maybe
meent	meant
meinister	minister
mem	ma'am
mester	master
micht	might
min'	mind
minit	minute
mither	mother
muckle	much
na	no, not
nae	no
nae odds	no difference
naethin'	nothing
nane	none
naw	not
neednae	needn't
nervis	nervous
nicht	night
niver	never
no	not
noo	now
nor	than

o'	of
ochanee, anee	an expression of weariness or lamentation
ocht	anything
ony	any
oor	our
oot	out
ornery	ordinary
ower	over
pit	put
poun'	pound(s)
power	lot
pu'	pull
puir	poor
pye	pay
quare	strange, unusual
quat	quit
Rabert	Robert
raised	excited
reddy	ready
rether	rather
richt	right
rin	run
rise	raise
sae	so
sair	sore
sang	blood
scaur	scare
shairly	surely
sherp	sharp
sheugh	ditch

shew	show
shud	should
shudna	shouldn't
sic	such
sich	such
skreghin'	screeching
soart	sort
soort	sort
sough	groaning sound
speek	speak
speerits	spirits
stanes	stones
stap	stop
stirk	young steer or bullock
suiner	sooner
sumbuddy	somebody
sumthin'	something
sune	soon
sur	sir
tabacca	tobacco
tae	to
tae	too
taen	taken
tak	take
talkit	talked
tap	top
tarble	terrible
taul'	told
tay	tea
tell't	told
terble	terrible
thae	those
thankit	thanked

the	they
the day	today
thocht	thought
till	to
tither	other
turmot	turnip
twa	two
wad	would
wae	way
waen	child
wark	work
warran'	warrant
wat	wet
waur	worse
waznae	wasn't
wee	small
weel	well
weemin	women
welkim	welcome
wha	who
whaur	where
wheen	number
whusky	whiskey
wi'	with
win'	wind
winnae	won't
wrang	wrong
wud	would
wudnae	wouldn't
wull	will
wuman	woman
wun'	wind
wundey	window

wunner	wonder
wur	were
wuz	was
ye	you
yer	you're
yer	your
yersel'	yourself
yin	one
yince	once
yis	yes

OTHER REPRINTS PUBLISHED BY BOOKS ULSTER

Betsy Gray or Hearts of Down ~ W. G. Lyttle

ISBN 978-1-910375-21-1

The Adventures of Paddy M'Quillan ~ W. G. Lyttle

ISBN: 978-1910375136

The Adventures of Robin Gordon ~ W. G. Lyttle

ISBN: 978-1910375150

Life in Ballycuddy, County Down ~ W. G. Lyttle

ISBN: 978-1910375174

Sons of the Sod: A Tale of County Down ~ W. G. Lyttle

ISBN: 978-1910375198

The Bush that Burned ~ Lydia Foster

ISBN: 978-1910375112

Popular Rhymes and Sayings of Ireland ~ John J. Marshall

ISBN: 978-1910375037

Sayings, Proverbs and Humour of Ulster ~ Sir John Byers

ISBN: 978-0954306380

Printed by Amazon Italia Logistica S.r.l.
Torrazza Piemonte (TO), Italy

68894829R00097